5|00
16.95

LUNENBURG

AN ILLUSTRATED HISTO

BRIAN CUTHBERTSON

FORMAC PUBLISHING COMPANY LIMITED
HALIFAX

The development and pre-publication work on this project was funded in part by the Canada/Nova Scotia
Cooperation Agreement on Cultural Development.
Formac Publishing Company Limited acknowledges the
support of the Canada Council and the Nova Scotia
Department of Education and Culture in the development of writing and publishing in Canada.

Canadian Cataloguing in Publication Data

Cutherbertson, Brian, 1936–

Lunenburg

Includes index.
ISBN 0-88780-358-X

1. Lunenburg (N.S.) — History. I. Title

FC2349.L85C87 1996   971.6'23
F1039.5.L9C87 1996

Formac Publishing Company Limited
5502 Atlantic Street
Halifax, Nova Scotia   B3H 1G4

Printed and bound in Canada

Photo Credits

Top=T, Centre=C, Bottom=B
Army Museum Halifax Citadel: p. 19(B);
Art Gallery of Nova Scotia p. 29;
Hugh A. Corkum Collection: pp. 3, 5, 7, 9, 13(T),14–24,
    26,27, 28(T), 29–33, 35, 36(B), 37, 39, 40, 41(C),
    42(B), 44(B), 46(C&B), 47, 49–51, 53, 55–57 (photo
    by Bob Brooks);
Elise Doane: p. iv;
Firefighters Museum, Dartmouth: p. 10;
Fisheries Museum of the Atlantic, Lunenburg: pp. 8, 11
    (photo by Knickle's Studio), 13 (photo by Knickle's
    Studio), 35 (photo by Knickle's Studio);
Estate of Jack Gray pp. 12 (courtesy the Sobey Art
    Foundation), 52 (courtesy Maritime Life Assurance
    Company);
Steven Isleifson: pp. i, v, vi, 61-64;
Knickle's Studio: pp. 19(T), 20(T), 21, 34, 42, 45(B), 54(T);
Lieutenant H. Pooley, William Inglis Morse Collection,
    Special Collections, Dalhousie University: pp. 1, 2, 6;
Lunenburg Academy Foundation: p. 54;
Public Archives of Nova Scotia: pp. 4, 30; Public Archives
    of Nova Scotia—Bailly Collection: pp. 14, 17(B),
    20(B), 23, 26, 28(T&B), 59; W.L. Bishop Collection:
    p. 16(B); Bollinger Collection: pp. 46, 48; Wallace
    MacAskill Collection: pp.15, 36, 38, 41(T)

CONTENTS

PREFACE

When James Lorimer and Carolyn MacGregor of Formac first approached me to write an illustrated history of Lunenburg, I did not hesitate to accept. Although I am not a native of the town, nor even a "come from away," I had come to know Lunenburgers and their history through my role as Head of Heritage for the Province from 1984 to 1995. The story of Lunenburg's Old Town becoming a World Heritage Site in 1995 was, from a professional viewpoint, history in the making. As an historian, I welcomed the opportunity to write the text for an illustrated history which would integrate visual and textual expression, each intimately complementing the other. My aim is to give the reader a more authentic feeling and understanding for the past than just words can accomplish. All historical writing is selective by nature, but illustrated history is particularly so. Its writing challenges an author to keep a judicious

balance between the powerful impressions images can give and the capability of words to communicate historical patterns of thought and action.

The waterfront in February

There is, I believe, a discernable historical pattern to be found in the nearly 250 years of Lunenburg's history as a fishing and seafaring community. This history began on June 8th, 1753 when 1,453 "foreign Protestants" sailed into Merligash Bay on Nova Scotia's South Shore to create new homes for themselves and their children. They came chiefly from farming districts drained by the Upper Rhine—the German Palatinate, French- and German-speaking Swiss cantons, and a small French-speaking princi-

pality, Montbéliard, adjoining Switzerland. This historical pattern derives its essence from succeeding generations inheriting two pre-eminent characteristic traits of the first settlers—their enterprise and solidity.

During researching and writing this book, I was continually struck by how Lunenburg merchants and fishermen have displayed these two traits at critical junctures in their town's history. These times have come when the town's fishing industry faced changes, often revolutionary in nature, in the harvesting and marketing of fish. Today, we place much emphasis on nurturing the relationship between local entrepreneurship and community development. There is no better illustration to be found of its worth to a

community than in the 250-year-history of Lunenburg Town.

Lunenburg's history divides readily into well-defined historical periods and these form the basis for chapters. Within chapters I have generally followed a sequence of describing change and adjustment in the fishing industry before turning to such various subjects of community life as elections, civic improvements, educational institutions, the role of churches, and sports and other pastimes. Lunenburgers answered the call to the colours in two world wars. In describing wartime Lunenburg, I have tried to balance the story of those who served overseas with the activities of those on the home front. Since the 1970s, preservation of Lunenburg heritage has become of growing concern to the town's citizens. In Chapter 5, I chart the rise of the heritage movement and tell the story of the Old Town becoming a World Heritage Site. The last chapter is a walking tour of the Old Town which I hope readers will feel encouraged to undertake.

Although many people have become involved in pre-serving Lunenburg's architectural heritage, I wish to dedicate this illustrated history to those I believe did the most to gain World Heritage Site status for the Old Town—successive Lunenburg Town Heritage Advisory Committees, Gordon Fulton of Parks Canada, William Plaskett formerly with the Lunenburg Planning Commission and now a heritage planner, and Lunenburg's deputy clerk, Peter Haughn. I also wish to dedicate this book to Hugh A. Corkum who has done so much to preserve the visual history of Lunenburg.

B. C.,
June 1996

These 19th century fish merchants' warehouses still serve Lunenburg's fishing industry.

Freeman-Blair House, 89 York Street

Chapter 1
1753-1853

"Nothing will give me greater pleasure than to hear that your Lordships have fallen upon some means of sending over German and other foreign Protestants." So wrote an increasingly frustrated Edward Cornwallis in his desire for honest and industrious settlers. As governor-in-chief of Nova Scotia, Cornwallis had brought out 2,500 settlers in 1749 to found Halifax and secure Nova Scotia as a British colony.

by the Upper Rhine—the German Palatinate, French- and German-speaking Swiss cantons, and Montbéliard, a small French-speaking principality adjoining Switzerland. They were among the thousands of mostly German Protestants who emigrated to the New World to escape oppressive taxation, religious persecution, fear of arbitrary impressment to fight foreign wars, and increasing overpopulation.

Well over half the foreign Protestants who came to Nova Scotia were farmers, but among them were carpen-

A view of Lunenburg from the south west by Lieutenant H. Pooley, 1816.

Most of them were drawn by promises of free rations for a year; they proved from the first a motley lot, worthless and lazy. There were, however, a few Swiss among them whom Cornwallis found honest and industrious, hence the plea to the Board of Trade in London.

"Their Lordships" obliged Cornwallis by sending out over 2,000 foreign Protestants between 1750 and 1752. These settlers came mainly from farming districts drained

ters, masons, bakers, shoemakers, tailors, butchers, and furriers. Most were Lutheran or French-speaking Swiss Calvinists. Many could read and write; a number of them had the benefits of an excellent education and they assumed leadership in local government and the nascent settlement's commercial life.

They arrived at Halifax during a brief uneasy peace in the continuing struggle between Britain and France for

North American empire. Settling them in agricultural townships among the Acadians on the Bay of Fundy side proved impossible as Cornwallis had insufficient military strength to ensure their security in the face of open French and Indian hostility. They languished in Halifax until finally in the spring of 1753, Cornwallis' successor as governor, Colonel Peregrine Hopson, abandoned the idea of settling them on the Bay of Fundy side. Instead, he chose the peninsula and lands around Merligash Bay on Nova Scotia's South Shore, a good day's sail from

throne for the Catholic Stuarts had only ended disastrously on the battlefield of Culloden seven years earlier. The British authorities never doubted that the foreign Protestants would be loyal subjects, despite significant differences in language and culture.

Settling the Town

Hopson gave command of the expedition settling Lunenburg to Colonel Charles Lawrence. In one of those

A view of Lunenburg from the south east by Lieutenant H. Pooley, c. 1820.

Halifax. This site offered better security, a well protected harbour, and what was believed to be the best fertile land on the colony's Atlantic coast.

Hopson gave the planned settlement the name of Lunenburg to honour King George II, who was also Duke of Brunschweig-Lüneburg, a German principality. In an age when one's religion generally determined one's loyalty to monarch and state, Hopson may well have thought his choice would reinforce the allegiance of these largely German settlers to the British Crown and the Protestant succession of the Hanoverian Georges; after all Bonnie Prince Charlie's attempt to regain the

fortunate occurrences for historians, Lawrence's journal of the first few days of the infant settlement and his letters to Hopson for the next two and half months were found and published in 1953. Although one of the leading settlers, Leonard Christopher Rudolf, wrote that they "went to work to clear the wilderness on the 7th June," we now know that the first of two flotillas bringing the 1,453 settlers did not leave Halifax until that evening. Lawrence's journal describes how they made an easy sail that night and: "At 7 [morning of the 8th June] came to an anchor in ye harbour of Merliguash… The last of ye Vessels came to an anchor at an hour after 9… At 11 ordered ye Regulars & militia and Rangers on shore, directing them to wait on ye beach, till I disembarked with ye settlers fit to bear arms."

Lawrence feared hostility to this expansion of British settlement especially as the government had reports that 300 Mi'kmaq were prepared to march as soon as they received knowledge of the expedition's departure. He gave priority to erecting defences which created, however, antagonism from many settlers who doubted any Indian menace. They were to be brutally disabused after war broke out with France two years later, in 1755, but meanwhile, as Lawrence told Hopson, the settlers were "inconceivably turbulent … and are only to be managed like a great ship in a violent storm, with infinite care, vigilance & attention."

By June 18 Surveyor General Charles Morris had laid out the town. On the following day the settlers took possession of their town lots for which they had earlier drawn. Morris's plan followed a town model provided by eighteenth-century British colonial authorities; two other North American examples, though by no means as intact as Lunenburg, are Halifax and Savannah, Georgia. Morris superimposed a rigid gridiron pattern of streets running from the harbour front up the steep hill to where the Academy building now stands. His plan provided for a parade, a space for public buildings, and an extensive belt of bordering common land. He marked off six divisions, each of which he divided into eight blocks with fourteen building lots per block. At just 40 by 60 feet deep, the small lots made for a highly compact town plan.

Rouche Brook, where first settlers landed, Lunenburg, Nova Scotia.—13.

Throughout the summer the settlers worked at clearing the forest and erecting huts and "good framed houses." Lawrence oversaw the completion of blockhouses and palisade before he left for Halifax in early September in order to succeed Hopson as governor. Lawrence left confident that he had dealt with the settlement's major problems. He was mistaken, however, for there was discontent and unhappiness over the distribution of government rations and supplies, and over Hopson's and Lawrence's decision not to subdivide the common land outside the immediate town boundaries, but to keep it intact for the whole community's future benefit. Many believed that the British government had not kept all of its promises. In December, some settlers attempted an armed rebellion. When a force arrived from Halifax, the rebels gave up and the "insurrection" was at an end. The government charged John William Hoffman with being the main instigator; he was tried, found guilty and punished with a £100 fine and two years' imprisonment. Today no one knows what actually transpired and what Hoffman's role was.

In 1754 many settlers moved out of the town to their 30-acre farm lots. The government also distributed livestock. In the town there were now 319 houses and 40 huts. The Board of Trade was becoming highly agitated over the settlement's mounting costs. Lawrence, often employing ingenious forms of deception on his superiors, convinced the Board to continue providing rations until 1760.

These first years in Lunenburg were lean and hard. The settlers were fearful of the Indian raids which reached their height during 1758. Concern for defence against possible Indian and French attack had caused Hopson to form a militia regiment before the settlers' departure from Halifax. All able-bodied men between the ages of 16 and 60 could be called out to serve in the Nova Scotian militia. Moreover, they had to arm themselves or suffer a penalty; for those unable to do so, the government provided muskets which the men could pay for by work or other means. Almost none of the 500 men in the Lunenburg settlement capable of bearing arms owned them. Somehow Hopson found the necessary muskets. He also took great care in the appointment of officers, seeking those with previous military experience. In Europe the Swiss had a reputation for being among finest soldiers and many left their homeland to serve in the armies of various monarchs. This may explain why Hopson gave a disproportionate number of officer commissions to the Swiss among the foreign Protestants. After Indians began killing settlers at their farms, the authorities had no choice but to deploy militia on the settlement's outskirts. Those called out received double pay of a shilling a day. In 1762 a threatened French naval attack on Halifax caused authorities to issue an order for the Lunenburg militia, along with other men from the recently settled New England Planter townships, to march to Halifax's defence. The continued fear of Indian raids so terrified the inhabitants that they petitioned for the men to remain and the order was rescinded.

By 1760 Lawrence could report that the settlers had "at length got the better of their greatest difficulties." Others commented on the "flourishing" state of the community and rapidly increasing population. A coasting

When the first settlers drew by lot for their grants of land, those conducting the draw wrote on the backs of playing cards, like this one for Creightons Division C No. 11, the names of the divisions and lot numbers.

trade developed, supplying Halifax with firewood and garden produce.   Lawrence had worked hard to ensure the infant settlement's success. He was able to call on it in 1758 for support in his struggle with Halifax's New England mercantile community over their demands for an elected Legislative Assembly. The merchants detested the autocratic Lawrence while he feared the threat of their dominance in an Assembly. Enlisted by Lawrence, Lunenburgers signed a petition opposing an elected Assembly. They feared, justifiably, that an Assembly under Halifax merchants' control would end government provisioning secured by Lawrence. However, the merchants carried the day and the Board of Trade ordered Lawrence to convene an Assembly.

The New Englanders petitioned London asking that the Lunenburgers be totally excluded from voting, arguing that they should not be classed as eligible voting freeholders, but as persons subsisting on charity. In an outlandish falsehood, these Halifax merchants described Lunenburg as settled by "Swiss Roman Catholics" and "Old Soldiers of the French Service." What really lay behind their opposition was the calculated fear that if the Lunenburg settlers had the right to vote, their numbers would permit them to dominate the election of members from the province at large. Worse still, they would elect representatives of Lawrence's choosing.

Few of the foreign Protestants had been naturalized; most had not been resident in North America for the required seven years. By the time of the 1758 election, at most half of the 250 adult males qualified for naturaliza-

A re-enactment around 1970 of the landing by the first settlers.

tion. Of these, 58 voted on July 31 for two township representatives and presumably for the 16 members elected for the province at large. They had the choice of seven candidates for the two townships seats; Alexander Kedy and Philip Knaut were easy winners. The Halifax mercantile oligarchy need not have worried about Lunenburg controlling the election for members at large; all 16 seats went to the merchants' candidates.

In the next decades Lunenburg grew steadily from the fruits of its trading relationship with Halifax. During the American Revolution, Lunenburg's increasing wealth

attracted Boston privateers who were plundering Nova Scotian towns as well as attacking British vessels. On July 1, 1783, about 90 of them attacked the unsuspecting town of 50 houses, plundering and burning at will. Townsmen were badly outnumbered with not more than 20 capable of bearing arms at the time. When Pastor Johann Schmeisser vigorously protested, the privateers bound and gagged him. Colonel John Creighton, a senior magistrate, and four others managed to secure the blockhouse. There was, however, only a small stock of powder and shot. A black servant of Creighton's, named Sylvia, carried powder in her apron, directly through the besieging Americans, "abusing and swearing at them as she passed along, and by her very effrontery and impudence, cleared her way," as Joseph Howe recounted the story in his newspaper the *Novascotian*.

Although the privateers fired over a hundred musket balls into the blockhouse walls, Colonel Creighton and those with him succeeded in killing seven or eight of the privateers before they brought up cannon and forced a surrender. During the firing, Colonel Creighton protected his small son by holding him between his feet. At a one point Sylvia also had to protect the lad by covering him with her body. Dettlieb Christopher Jessen defended his house until he was able to escape by the back door and leave the town in order to rally the militia. Because Jessen fired on them, the privateers took everything in the house, leaving him with no more than the clothes on his back. After plundering anything of value, amounting to £8,000 worth, the assailants threatened to burn every building unless the people paid a ransom. Some agreed to pay £1,000, but Colonel Creighton "tauntingly" refused. They burnt his house, seized £3,300 in property and took him to Boston where he remained unflinching as ever until the peace.

During the long war with Revolutionary and Napoleonic France which began in 1793, the government gave the militia more resources than it ever had since Hopson's day or would ever again. Colonel John Creighton was in command. The town secured cannon, muskets, powder and shot from Halifax. When the War of 1812 with the United States broke out, fear of privateers was once again uppermost in the minds of the town's inhabitants. The first blockhouses had fallen into

A manuscript map of Lunenburg drawn by Lieutenant H. Pooley, c. 1821

decay so new ones were erected, one on Blockhouse Hill and a second at the old Fort Boscawen guarding the harbour's entrance.

The fortunes of war did not favour Lunenburg when it came to privateering. Although the town was not invaded again, American privateers captured a number of Lunenburg vessels at great loss to the town's merchants. A group of merchants purchased, in Halifax, a captured American privateer which they named the *Lunenburg*. She had considerable success as a privateer, but her captures never redeemed for her owners their earlier losses.

At the end of the war, the town quickly recovered and entered an era of solid, steady prosperity. By 1830 two dozen stores lined its waterfront selling British manufactures and West Indian goods. Such merchant families as the Rudolfs, Ernsts, Oxners, and Zwickers built up a trade by exchanging cargoes of fish in the West Indies and South America, for rum, sugar and molasses. They brought these north to sell in Halifax, Quebec, and Newfoundland. An annual export of 25,000 quintals of codfish was usual. Local garden produce and cattle also found a ready market in Newfoundland. English demand for Lunenburg lumber employed yet more shipping. The town could boast more than 15 square-rigged vessels with a combined tonnage of 1500 tons. Around 100 coasters found ready employment in carrying firewood and agricultural products to Halifax and in the Labrador fishery.

This mercantile wealth remained within the town and county and proved to be the community's major economic strength. The youthful editor of the *Novascotian*, Joseph Howe, remarked on how much

Lunenburgers exemplified "the virtues of steady perseverance and systematic economy." As a consequence they lived in comfort, many had acquired no mean fortunes and few were in debt. It was not an uncommon occurrence at a householder's death to find one or two thousand pounds in specie in his chest.

The only critical note in Howe's observations was the habit of Lunenburgers to front their houses along the street line, instead of having front gardens and tree lines as in other provincial towns. But he and other visitors noted approvingly that the town of 1,100 had a "lively and prosperous" air, boasting nearly 150 houses, many neatly painted in such "whimsical" colours as pink, red and even green as well as white. There were three churches, their spires shooting skyward, and several stores and public buildings including a courthouse.

Early 19-century jug belonging to the merchant John Joseph Rudolph

Politics

From the first elections after Lunenburg's founding through to the winning of responsible government nearly a century later, the town's leading families—principally the Creightons, Rudolfs, Kaulbachs, and Zwickers—formed a family compact as closely knit as any in the province. These families and others, such as those of Philip Knaut and John Heckman, were determined to keep Assembly representation for both the town and the county firmly in their own hands. Although Charles Lott Church of Chester succeeded in taking one of the two county seats in 1820 and holding it in the 1826 election, the family compact secured his defeat in 1830 by shrewdly arranging for a second candidate from Chester who split that township's vote. This allowed William Rudolf and

John Creighton (grandson of the colonel) to take the two county seats while John Heckman went in unopposed for the town.

The significant role that the fishery, shipping and West Indian trade now played in the economic life of Lunenburg could not be better illustrated than by the bloc voting of its members. Although most of their constituents still relied on farming as the basis of their livelihood, the three Lunenburg members voted consistently for measures advantageous to the fishery while opposing those designed to benefit agriculture. Close commercial ties between the leading Lunenburg families and Halifax's ruling oligarchy had been a constant factor in the town's politics. As the movement for political reform gathered momentum, a natural alliance of commercial interests now became a common political front. In the last session leading up to the pivotal 1836 election, Heckman, Rudolf, and Creighton all voted against any reform measures that challenged the hold the oligarchy had on the colony's political life. Then in the 1836 election Nova Scotian politics were transformed almost overnight when a new party, the Reformers (later called Liberals), triumphed over the Tories.

For this election Church, as a Reformer, was determined to re-enter the Assembly; the compact was equally determined to deny him a seat. After the Chester polling Church led by a wide margin—184 votes to Creighton's 37 and Rudolf's 22. However, at the

Lunenburg town poll he faced the worst violence ever experienced to that date in a county election. The "rabble," as Charles Lott Church called them, led by the legal fraternity, abetted by the principal merchants and shopkeepers, employed "shameful strategems." Creighton's and Rudolf's open houses provided rum laced with molasses that was used in the making of spruce beer, thus much increasing its potency. Such confusion reigned that a boxing match broke out on the courthouse floor where the polling was taking place. After five days of polling and another day at Petite Riviere, Creighton and Rudolf overcame Church's early lead and triumphed.

The town's Tory compact was in full control until the 1847 election. This election was fought over the issue of responsible government. There was every reason to believe that the governing Conservatives could count on electing three members from Lunenburg. It was not to be. Reasons for the sudden and surprising Tory collapse are not entirely clear but can be attributed to the Liberal leader Joseph Howe's determined campaigning in the county. To his own and the Liberals' amazement, Howe found that there was no county where his popularity was "higher or more universal" than in Lunenburg. The upshot was a complete Liberal victory and an end to the Tory "reign of terror" in Lunenburg and the collapse of the compact of the leading families.

A colonial banks schooner, c. 1830

Health in the New Town

Among the earliest settlers there were no less than eight physicians, both military and civilian. They were Leonard Lockman, Johann Erad, J. Ulrich Klett, Johann Carl Deglen, Christopher Nicolai, Johann Edmund, John Phillips and John Baxter. Even so, the lack of a midwife

and high infant mortality were matters of great concern. Lawrence obtained a further £10 for the settlement in order that a midwife could be engaged. In 1767, Maria Moser and Maria Tattray each received £5 as midwives. In addition, John Phillips told the Halifax authorities in 1759 that he was acting as a man-midwife. Since the early part of the eighteenth century, men-midwives had increasingly attended at births because they used forceps, which the midwives had not adopted. There was a small birthing hospital in Lunenburg: in a return of births there was a notation, "14 births in the Hospital which has five cradles." By 1760 the only physicians left were Phillips and Johann Carl Deglen. Phillips departed six years later for England because of ill health.

In the eighteenth century, no disease was dreaded more than smallpox. Nova Scotia experienced its first major outbreak in 1775. It appeared first in Halifax causing the Assembly to enact a law requiring those infected or recently inoculated be quarantined. They were to hang a flag outside their house and remain inside until the infection passed. By late summer it reached Lunenburg. The Reverend Peter DelaRoche inoculated his eldest child, which suggests that there was no longer a physician in the town. He estimated that more than 1,000 had become infected but only 80 had died. Although smallpox appeared in Lunenburg again in 1800, 1827, 1874, and 1877, the 1775 outbreak seems to have been the worst.

In the aftermath of the American Revolution, among the dozen British army surgeons who came to Nova Scotia was John Bolman, surgeon to General de Riesdesel's Hessian regiment. Bolman settled at Lunenburg where he married Philip Knaut's widow and rapidly rose in prominence. In the 1793 election Bolman defeated a challenge for the Township seat in the Assembly by a young lawyer, Lewis Morris Wilkins, a scion of the Shelburne Wilkins family. Infuriated by his loss, Wilkins and four others attacked Bolman's house and apothecary shop, breaking windows, smashing over a hundred medicine bottles, and rendering the house and shop uninhabitable. Bolman proved to be an active Assembly member, remaining in the legislature until 1809. He lived in Lunenburg practising medicine until his death in 1833.

The *Novascotian* took particular note in 1845 of an operation by Lunenburg's Dr. William Slocumb employing mesmerism. After putting a 14-year-old boy into a hypnotic state, he corrected the boy's club foot. As the paper noted with approbation, "the Doctor has made a capital job of it—in fact, he made a perfect fit of it." The boy felt no pain. Slocumb had taken the boy into his home for the operation and done it without charge.

Education

German long remained the first language for many Lunenburg residents. Evidently, most adults could read and write, though there was no free schooling in Nova Scotia until 1864. For the merchant and professional class there was the Lunenburg Academy, mostly supported by parent subscriptions and a small government grant. Its annual public examination, held in the presence of School Commissioners, members of the Legislature, and parents, was an occasion of note. Latin and various forms of English education, including geometry and the use of globes were part of the curriculum. By 1836 it had 77

scholars apparently taught by a single teacher, William Lawson. There were also four schools for poor children, maintained by private subscription, with 90 students in all. These were kept by Mary Harley, Elizabeth Watson, Hannah Bryzelius and Lucy Metzler, described in the school returns as "deserving females." In 1833 citizens got their first public library; two years later the Reverend James Cochran noted it had 300 volumes.

ST. JOHN'S CHURCH, LUNENBURG, N. S.
Originally built by the Imperial Government in 1754

Churches

The German-speaking foreign Protestants brought with them both Lutheranism and Presbyterianism in the form of the Dutch Reformed Church, while French-speaking Montbéliardians were Lutherans, the French-speaking Swiss, Calvinists, and the few English, Anglicans. Language of service, the liturgy and doctrine were highly contentious issues. Until the completion of St. John's Anglican Church in 1754, the town's first minister, the Reverend Jean Baptiste Moreau, preached in the open in both English and French. His colleague, a Swede by birth, the Reverend Paulius Bryzelius, preached in English and German; his sermons were so moving, reported a Lunenburg official to the lieutenant governor, they caused many to shed tears. The church galleries were often crowded and in danger of collapsing. Peter DelaRoche, a native of Geneva who arrived after Bryzelius, could preach in all three languages.

Initially, three denominations used St. John's for their services. Then the Presbyterians erected their own church in 1769 and secured the services of Bruin Romcas Comingo. Dutch by birth, his 1770 ordination at Halifax's St. Matthew's was the first for Protestants in Canada. For many years, women sat on the ground floor; the men sat in the gallery. The elders and deacons sat on either

Lunenburg Town's Fire Engine of 1842, now on display at the Firefighters' Museum, Yarmouth

side of the pulpit. The unmarried sat on one side of the church and the married on the other.

Lutherans first secured a minister in 1772 with the arrival of the Reverend Frederick Schultz, who preached his first sermon in the newly constructed church, built largely with voluntary labour. At the rising of the frame the church provided workmen with 11 gallons of rum and 20 gallons of spruce beer. Schultz dedicated the church as Zion Evangelical Lutheran Church. The congregations purchased the chapel bell from the old Fortress Louisbourg, and it first rang from the new church on August 11, 1776.

When the Presbyterian minister James Munro visited Lunenburg in 1795, he found the Lutherans the most numerous, followed by the Calvinists of the Dutch Reformed Church, and then the Anglicans. German was the language of service for the first two. The French-speaking Calvinists had generally become Anglican.

During the first half of the nineteenth century, the churches went from strength to strength under such outstanding clergy as Ferdinand Conrad Temme and Adam Moschell, both from Germany, and James Cochran, who was among the first to take up the temperance cause, though not without having to face much ridicule.

Community Pastimes

Lunenburg had a range of community pastimes, including theatrical entertainments. A Halifax correspondent reported attending the plays "Paul Pry" and "Village Lawyer." He noted how pleased he had been by the taste, skill, and order which were so conspicuous at the Lunenburg entertainment. Another correspondent to a Halifax newspaper provided readers in February 1830 with a daily weather chart for the previous year and its impact on social life. He commented that so far that winter the temperature had dipped below freezing only three times; it had been so mild that there had not been a day's sleighing, which was "without precedent in the meteorological history of the Country." If such outdoor activity became impossible, there were numerous "gatherings" during the long winter. On a January night in 1842 the Crown Fire Company gathered at Mrs. Oxner's, where the tables displayed every "luxury an epicure could desire." After dinner, there were songs, duets and glees, wine flowed in abundance and the "evening passed off with the greatest hilarity."

Weddings were another opportunity for enjoyable festivities. On the wedding day the party, led by the bride and groom, walked to the church. The women dressed in white with white caps decorated with ribbons while the men wore white trousers and round blue jackets. After the church service, the party would adjourn to a tavern for the wedding feast. For years a custom persisted of removing one of the bride's slippers while she was at the table and then passing it around for guests to deposit coins as a gift to her. For several days afterwards there was dancing and other amusements.

Centenary

Lunenburg started its second century on June 7, 1853, beginning day-long celebrations with a 25-gun salute from Barrack Hill. The Centenary Prayer, with its splendidly moving words, "O Lord, when we look back on this century now closing, how great has been Thy goodness to us and our forefathers," gave thankful voice to the descendants of those foreign Protestants who had forsaken their homelands for a new life in Nova Scotia.

Chapter 2

1853-1913

A s Lunenburg entered its second century, few believed the town was on the threshold of its most expansive era. In the 1850s Lunenburgers were in a "slough of despond", caused by the severest depression of the century, compounded by Britain's move to free trade and the end of preferential treatment for colonial shipping. Lunenburg's West Indian trade and fish exports declined drastically. The town's foreign trade fell into the hands of Halifax's "Merchant Princes." Led by James Eisenhauer in the 1860s, however, Lunenburg merchants such as W.N. Zwicker and Lewis Anderson aggressively sought new foreign markets.

When the American Civil War broke out in 1861, the North put in place a naval blockade of southern ports. This gave rise to an immediate demand for vessels with captains bold enough to run the blockade. The risks were great, but so were the rewards, with goods being sold at six and seven times their cost to Lunenburg merchants. The resulting wealth became a crucial factor for the town's recovery from the mid-century depression. Some of this wealth went for purchasing 59 lots of common land. This created a building boom that established New Town. From the 1860s on the term "Old Town" referred to the original settlement.

Above and left: A salt bank schooner on the banks around 1900. At the end of the day the dories have returned to the schooner with their catch. This model from the Lunenburg Fisheries Museum shows some of the crew unload fish and grear, and hoisting the dories aboard. The fish splitting crew is hard at work on the catch.

"Doreymen off Canso Bank," by Jack Gray, is owned by the Sobey Art Foundation.

For the fishing industry a decisive turning point came in 1873. Five vessels went to the Grand Banks off Newfoundland but four crews became disheartened with the fishing and abandoned the banks for their usual Labrador fishery. Captain Benjamin Anderson stayed. Instead of the traditional handlining, he employed a new technology of trawling and brought home a significantly increased catch. The famous Lunenburg "banks" fishery was born, and by century's end, it employed some 2,000 men in 180 vessels.

On the first Sabbath proceeding March 21, the town's churches held special services for the departing fleet's first trip to the banks. "Eternal Father, Strong to Save," and "Fierce Raged the Tempest O'er the Deep" were among the favourite hymns. On the next day, the fleet was a proud sight as it set sail and departed en masse.

A year's work for a typical 90-ton Lunenburg schooner with her captain and 17-man crew, some as young as 16 years old, began in early spring with loading supplies and gaspereau bait. From her home port she headed for the western banks near treacherous Sable Island, a fisherman's "mecca" in the early spring. After fishing for some weeks she might go next to the Magdalene Islands to procure herring bait and then head for Banquero Bank off Canso.

Once at their chosen fishing grounds, the crew set out trawls, baited hooked lines a mile to a mile and a half in length. Two-man dories visited the trawls three or four times before salting the day's catch of cod. It was hard and dangerous work, for dories could become lost in the fog for days or be swamped. After six weeks or so, she would return to Lunenburg to unload. Almost immediately she set sail again this time for the Grand Banks, collecting bait at Burin, Caplin Bay or St. Marys in Newfoundland. Three months on the Grand Banks was the usual stay before returning home to unload towards the end of September. Workers at the fish curing stores along the town's waterfront gave the catches the "Lunenburg cure." The

Fishermen's Valentine

town's merchant firms found a ready market for the cured cod in the Caribbean.

The money from the season's catch of cod, haddock, hake, and halibut was divided equally among the crew, with individuals earning as much as $300. After a thorough cleaning, many schooners engaged in freighting during the winter months. Runs could take them to the United States, the West Indies, South America, and sometimes the Mediterranean, but they always ensured they were ready for the first spring trip.

Shipbuilding revived with the bank fishery. By late 1880s the town could boast 17 square-riggers engaged in international commerce. The Young, Morash, and Smith families became leading shipbuilders. Among the more famous was the *Sceptre*, owned by Zwickers, which in 1888 made the round voyage to Puerto Rico and the Turks' Islands and back to Lunenburg in 32 days. She also made eight round-trip voyages to the West Indies inside of 14 months. Another, the *Geneva*, built by James Maxner, made the passage from Halifax around the Cape Horn to Vancouver in 110 days and broke all sailing records to the Pacific port. By the turn of the century, Lunenburg was second to Halifax and ahead of Yarmouth and Windsor

This photograph of Zwicker & Company's buildings and wharf was taken around 1900

in having 296 registered vessels. She was the least of the four, however, in total tonnage because so much of the Lunenburg fleet was of the fishing schooner class.

A Half Century of Prosperity

By 1867 townspeople were feeling more confident in their prospects than they had for several decades, which may be why the Halifax *British Colonist* reported that the celebrations for Lunenburg's first Dominion Day

"eclipsed all previous displays." At sunrise the Volunteer Artillery Company marched to Gallows Hill where they fired a 21-gun salute and the church bells rang out. At noon, Sheriff John Kaulbach, in his official uniform, read the Queen's Proclamation for the new Dominion to a salute of 50 guns. The crowd sang the "God Save the Queen" after which school children gave voice to an ode appropriate for the occasion. Sheriff Kaulbach then led the assembly in three cheers. In the afternoon, the infantry volunteers held a rifle practice and the day's celebrations ended with another 21-gun salute.

The town was basking in prosperity. In 1888 the *Lunenburg Progress* boasted that a "cool" million had been amassed by the town's industries. Her shipyards had launched 13 new vessels worth $70,000. Moreover, her fish exports had amounted to nearly $800,000, while the value of new buildings constructed had come to $32,000, coopering was worth another $12,000, and a further $8,000 had come from the construction of small boats. Her fishing fleet exceeded 100 vessels and provided employment for 2,000 men. In fact, since the 1860s the town had nearly doubled the number of its buildings, quadrupled in wealth and greatly increased in population. Property values were on a par with Halifax.

The town's historian, H.W. Hewitt, declared the eight years since Queen Victoria's Golden Jubilee in 1887 were the "most momentous in the modern history of the town." Lunenburg celebrated this occasion with its usual gusto and fanfare. It was also the summer when Lunenburg

yacht, *Esme*, defeated the best of Halifax's Nova Scotia Yacht Squadron to bring home the Marquis of Lorne Cup.

Other than industries directly connected to the fishery and shipbuilding as coopering and block and sail making, the town could not boast any domestic manufacturing until 1874. That year Frank Powers began producing mechanical fog alarms, ship signals, lanterns, as well as bicycles and hot water heating apparatuses.

In the 1880s J. Rafuse began making carriages and sleighs and the Lunenburg Furniture Company opened. But the 1891 incorporation of the Lunenburg Iron

Above: Fish processing workers on the Lunenburg Waterfront, 1900. Inset: The noted photographer Wallace MacAskill took this view of Smith and Rhuland's Shipyard during the building of Bluenose which is on the stocks in the foreground.

Foundry, equipped with the most advanced machinery and occupying over 12,000 square feet of space, marks the first major manufacturing operation. It produced all kinds of cooking and heating stoves, ship castings in brass and iron, mill and general machinery, bells weighing from 100 to 700 pounds, and marine engines. A 1906 fire nearly proved disastrous for the foundry, but John James Kinley organized a company to buy the firm and it survived.

Improvements within the town were matched by new communications to the outside world. The steamship, *City of Saint John*, made weekly trips between Yarmouth and Halifax calling at Lunenburg. The Lunenburg Steam Packet Company put into service the S.S. *Lunenburg* commanded by Captain R. Heisler, one of the best pilots on the South Shore. It alternated a daily service to Halifax with the S.S. *Bridgewater*. In the summer months the ships made calls at Chester. After much refinancing, the inducements of government subsidies and changes in ownership, the last rail was laid in 1889 for the Nova Scotia Central Railway. It ran from Middleton in the Annapolis Valley to Lunenburg. The steamship and rail services (in 1913 the South Shore Railway began

The Lunenburg Foundry Band posed for this photograph, probably at the 1920 Foundry picnic. Top row: Jim Young, Roy Maxner, Evrett Rafuse, Clayton Tobin, Harold Bazel Smith, Dan Young, Dan Eisnor, J.J. Kinley, Ray Schwartz, Roy Schwartz, Freeman Corkum, Doug Silver, Judson Pyke, Nathan Young. Sitting: Lemuel Schwartz, Bernie Lohnes, Willis Zinck, Charlie Gustavan, Jimmy Hall, Lorne Nichols, Albert Young, Victor Corkum, Billy Whynacht, Mark Tobin, Charlie Miller, Freeman Glasgow, Ira MacCharicon. Lying down: Leslie Hall, Clyde Schwartz. Right: Fish drying on flakes around 1900

The Train Station around 1910

operation) launched the town's tourism industry.

In 1892 the Oddfellows drew 3,000 to their picnic at Kaulbach's Head; they came by rail from the Annapolis Valley, and by steamship from Halifax and along the South Shore. The Halifax *Morning Herald* reported that they found the town with its residences "models of taste and neatness," giving evidence of culture and luxury. Nearly all were made attractive by bright displays of flowers. Private houses, hotels and public buildings vied with each other "to please the eye and the nostril." At Kaulbach's Head, a beautiful tract of land on the harbour's other side,

Colonel Charles Kaulbach continued to make yearly improvements to what had become a public park.

For Queen Victoria's Diamond Jubilee in 1897, citizens put up two evergreen arches on Lincoln Street adorned with patriotic inscriptions. The grand parade and other events over the two days drew thousands from the Annapolis Valley by special trains and from along the South Shore. Eight hundred children marched through town singing patriotic songs. An athletic meet drew 1,200 people. The fire engine, beautifully decorated and the hose reels carrying "daintily white-

Lunenburg celebrates in 1897 Queen Victoria's Diamond Jubilee. Below: Militia Encampment at Blockhouse Hill in 1909

clad girls drawn by uniformed firemen" were the high points of an evening's torch-lit procession. A.E. Cogswell wrote a special hymn, "Canada's Jubilee Prayer." Many came to hear the Lunenburg's famous bands, the inheritance of a rare musical tradition.

Militia

Militia volunteers played a leading role in the town during the period. During the American Civil War a number of serious incidents on the high seas between British and American vessels gave rise to an increasingly belligerent Northern attitude towards the British North American colonies. Fear of invasion by Northern forces led to the formation of the British North American colonial volunteer movement. In 1862, 100 Lunenburgers came forward to form a volunteer company, which held its first target practice and inspection later in the year. Other townsmen formed a volunteer artillery company.

In 1866 fear of attack from Irish nationalists in United States, the Fenians, who were threatening to invade British North America, led to a call out of the volunteers. On the high hills between the LaHave River and Lunenburg, wood stood piled ready to be lit in a sequence of warning bonfires. The Fenian scare became an important factor for promoting Confederation and Nova Scotia's momentous decision to join the new nation of Canada.

One of the first acts of the new Dominion Government was a thorough militia reorganization. In 1870 it authorized the 75th Lunenburg Volunteer Battalion of Infantry, with its regimental headquarters and four of its companies in the town.

For training, the volunteers used the Drill Shed, which had its own colourful history. Around 1840 some citizens had the building's frame constructed in Boston, then stripped down and shipped to Lunenburg for erection. It remained under private management until the turn of the century when the Department of Militia and Defence officially took possession, renaming it the Armouries. The old Drill Shed served many purposes. During winter it became a skating rink and in the warmer months hosted vaudeville troupes. In 1895 it was crammed to the rafters for a fight between the colourful Paddy Ryan and the finest and toughest boxer of the time, John L. Sullivan.

Colonel Edwin Kaulbach, M.P.

Politics

At the time of Confederation, Lunenburg County became a single seat constituency in the new Dominion Parliament. The Liberals, running as anti-Confederates and led by Joseph Howe in his campaign to obtain better terms for Nova Scotia, dominated with little opposition from the beleaguered Conservatives. Edward McDonald took the seat for the Liberals in 1867 election. In the 1872 and 1874 elections Charles Edward Church, a grandson of Charles Lott Church who had suffered at the hands of the town's family compact, held the seat without difficulty for the Liberals.

For both the Liberals and Conservatives the great issue of the day was trade relations with the United

States. During the 1870s Canada was in the midst of a depression. Before going down to defeat in 1872, the Conservatives had attempted but failed to negotiate a reciprocity treaty (free trade) with the United States. The incoming Liberals tried as well, but the American Congress was more interested in raising than lowering tariffs. Opposition to free trade grew apace, especially among Ontario manufacturers. Sir John A. Macdonald and his Conservatives saw their opportunity. While the Liberals continue to uphold the principles of free trade, the Conservatives embraced protectionism. In the election held on September 17, 1878, they swept back into power. Macdonald launched his National Policy of protectionism against American imports, a policy that was to remain a pillar of Canadian economic policy until the 1988 North American Free Trade Agreement.

In the 1878 election Charles Church stood with his party on free trade. His opponent, wealthy shipowner and commanding officer of the 75th Volunteer Battalion Colonel Charles Edwin Kaulbach seems not to have campaigned on protection at all. Instead he attacked the Liberals for high taxes and assailed Church personally. In what became a pattern, Kaulbach took all the Lunenburg town polls.

In 1882 the federal and provincial elections were held on the same date. Instead of standing for the federal seat, Church ran successfully for the House of Assembly where he remained until 1902 when he was elevated to the Senate. The Liberals put up Thomas Keefler to oppose Kaulbach. Keefler won, but his election was disallowed and he lost in a by-election to Kaulbach.

Although the Conservatives won the 1887 national election, in Lunenburg, Liberal James Eisenhauer triumphed by 122 votes. A merchant whose fish export business was among the largest in the Maritimes, he had sat in the provincial Assembly from 1867 to 1878. Eisenhauer strongly opposed Macdonald's National Policy of protecting home industry and campaigned for free

JAMES D. EISENHAUER. M.P.
PRESENTED BY "LUNENBURG PROGRESS"

CANADA POST C

THE ADDRESS ONLY TO BE WRITTEN O

The Town Hall and Court House in 1910. Inset top left: James Eisenhauer, M.P.

trade with the United States. He did so again when an exhausted and dying Macdonald fought the 1891 election on opposition to reciprocity, rallying his party with the cry "The Old Man, the Old Flag, and the Old Policy."

During this election, Lunenburgers had the added excitement of two highly partisan newspapers. *The Progress* stood four square for the Liberals and reciprocity, while the *Argus* weighed in for the Conservatives. *The Progress* offered any new subscriber, and those who would pay what they owed, a picture of James Eisenhauer. It was "no common picture" announced the editor, but "a first class production on one of the best chisels on this continent, and if neatly framed, will add to the lustre of the best furnished rooms." In five weeks the *Progress* claimed it had given away 500 pictures. Kaulbach not only swept the town polls again, but also did well enough in the county at large to defeat Eisenhauer by 190 votes. After Kaulbach's resounding victory, the Liberal Progress offered his picture on the same terms as it had Eisenhauer's!

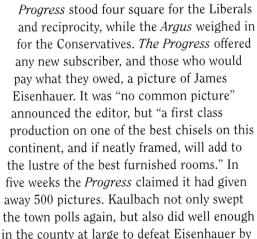

The next great contest was the 1911 election in which Sir Wilfred Laurier's governing Liberals once more made reciprocity their main platform. Robert Borden and his Conservatives met the challenge head on—reciprocity meant Canada's absorption by the United States. In

Constructing the Town Hall in 1891.

Diamond Jubilee Parade lining up outside of St. Andrew's Presbyterian Church and Sunday School Hall

Lunenburg the Tories did better than in any previous election as Dugald Stewart, a Bridgewater physician, easily defeated John Sperry by 379 votes. As usual the town's polls were all for the Conservatives.

Incorporation and Town Improvements

In 1888 the Legislative Assembly passed the Towns Incorporation Act, which allowed for elective municipal government to replace the old system of Halifax-appointed justices of the peace. After a short, hard struggle, Lunenburg ratepayers voted for incorporation. As the "friends of incorporation" had a "ticket" of candidates, endorsed by a hundred ratepayers, ready for new council election, the *Progress* editor wrote with confidence that there would be no election. Incorporation opponents supposedly had agreed that only those favourable should be elected, so they would have ample chance to prove incorporation was not a "snare and delusion." However, this editorializing by a "stranger" greatly offended the opponents who now put up an opposing slate.

The two mayoralty candidates were Augustus Wolff, who favoured incorporation, and J. Joseph Rudolf, an opposer. Wolff was a native of Stralsund in Prussia,

Water Street, Lunenburg, N. S.

Germany. After receiving his master's certificate at Liverpool, England, he had come to Bridgewater as mate on a vessel. He then succeeded to the command of a number of vessels before deciding to settle in Lunenburg. Rudolf was a scion of one of the town's leading families.

When it came time for Sheriff Creighton to count the votes, there was a large and eager crowd in attendance in the Court House. Creighton counted the mayor's ballot box first; the totals were Rudolf with 136 and Wolff, 135—for a total of 271 ratepayers voting. Then the clerk noted with consternation that he had listed in the poll book only 268 names. The ballot box had clearly been "stuffed" with three extra ballots. Sheriff Creighton proceeded to return all the ballots to the box and shake it well before withdrawing three random ballots. The three, however, were all for Rudolf so he lost three from his total. This gave the election to Wolff. All the aldermanic candidates favourable to incorporation gained election. So ended Lunenburg Town's first municipal election.

The town's by-laws divided it into three wards. Ward 1 contained all the town between the front and back harbours, lying south-east of line through King Street. From this line to the north-western boundary line of the original town plot composed Ward 2. The remainder lay in Ward 3. The new by-laws included provisions concerning the firing of guns, unusual noises, furious driving and coasting, and the prevention of vice.

Increasing wealth and a flourishing civic spirit gave impetus to an era of improvements undreamt of a few years before. Even before incorporation the Marine Hospital had been completed, a telephone system installed with 50 subscribers, and E.L. Nash had established the Maritimes' first incandescent lighting plant. The death of a volunteer firefighter in an 1885 fire caused a ratepayers meeting to give authority to purchase a new steam fire engine. But the big debate was over the installation of a modern water supply system. Lunenburg may have been first with electricity, but it was to be nearly last in getting a water supply. Many of the older generation felt that wells and the gathering of rain water were sufficient. Although a water company put forth a stock prospectus in the late 1880s, it made no headway. A *Progress* editorial, ever strong in the temperance cause, remarked the prospectus was an "immense" step; there was "a cold logic about the idea of bringing in water and driving out whisky, which speaks volumes for the mental and moral calibre" of Lunenburgers. By a majority of twelve ratepayers, the town finally got authority in 1893 to install a water supply system.

In March 1890, W.H. Smith arrived in the town with an offer to introduce a house numbering system and publish a directory. However, the Town Council did not consider house numbering came under its civic responsibilities. Nevertheless, the numbering went ahead and property owners paid Smith 50 cents for a white nickel-plated house number. At the same time street signs were erected. Under a 1901 Act, if property owners were prepared to pay half the cost, they could have the town pave their streets.

Churches

During the last half of the nineteenth century the Town's churches were remodelled, enlarged, or new ones built. The Lutherans replaced their first church in 1841 with a larger building adorned with a striking steeple. Inside were the traditional pews, balconies running the length of each side of the

Lincoln Street in summer and in a snowy winter around the turn of century. There were many complaints about the failure of citizens to clear snow from the streets in front of their establishments and residences.

nave and an imposing wine-glass pulpit. Of the old church they kept only the key and the money chest which had come from Germany with the original settlers. Fastened with three locks, it was four feet long by fifteen inches wide, made of very hard wood lined with iron. Each Sunday parishioners put their collection through a hole in the cover. The congregation continued to use the beautiful communion table plate set presented in 1814 by Christopher Jessen.

In this period Lutherans were blessed with the Reverend Doctor Charles Ernest Cossmann as their pastor. In 1876 he resigned to become a missionary within the county. He was a graduate of the Halle University, Germany, and preached his first sermon in Zion Lutheran on the fourth Sunday of January 1835. During his ministry, he baptised 3,966 persons, married 622 couples, buried 1,041 corpses, and preached 11,000 sermons. He lived to see Lutherans erect a third church in 1890, the present Zion Evangelical Lutheran. The greatest occasion of his ministry came when the church celebrated the 350th anniversary of Martin Luther's presentation of the Augsburg Confession. At the service the grey-haired and venerable pastor ascended the pulpit he had preached from for 41 years to read, in the original German, the Augsburg Confession. Though few of the younger generation could understand him, many of the older members of the congregation could. After his death the congregation dedicated a window in his remembrance. It has a cross at the top and below a copy of Luther's statue with the words:

Hier stehe ich, ich
Kann nicht anders.
Rev. C.E. Cossmann, D.D.

St. John's was remarkably transformed from a small meeting house into the much enlarged and architecturally arresting Victorian Gothic church that we see today. In the 1870s, under the direction of Halifax architects Stirling and Dewar, the church was remodelled, extended and expanded. Towards the end of the 1880s the congregation had Solomon Morash, a communicant and master craftsman, employ carpenter shipwrights to enlarge the chancel and put in new aisles. These renovations from the 1870s created one of the most beautiful church interiors in Nova Scotia with its lofty native pine ceiling and the enriched and pronounced Gothic features. The result is Carpenter-Gothic style at its finest.

Lunenburg has the oldest tradition of interior decorative painting in the province, so it is not surprising that the painting done in this period inside St. John's remains so brilliant in its effect. The famous chimes were a gift of Charles Edwin Kaulbach. Menuly Company of West Troy, New York, made the ten chimes, weighing in total 8,000 pounds, using a new process of toning and attuning involving the "most perfect acoustics." The Kaulbach family also presented the five stained glass windows that so splendidly light and grace the chancel.

In 1879 the Presbyterians undertook a thorough remodelling of their church. This was the year that the Reverend William Duff retired from the pastorate after 36 years of service. One sermon, affectionately delivered and well remembered, was for the burial of a lady in his congregation who had died aged 102 years. He chose as his text "This I say brethren, the time is short." He was also a noted agriculturist and for many years a member of the Lunenburg Agricultural Society. In a most moving ceremony in 1909, Lunenburg Presbyterians unveiled three magnificent stained-glass windows to the memory of William Duff, to their first minister Bruin Comingo, and to James Eisenhauer, a long-time elder.

View in the 1880s of the Old Academy Building erected in 1865 on the Parade. Right: School children in the 1890s.

The Methodists' first church dated from 1816. Although they later enlarged it, the need for a more substantial structure became apparent. In 1883 Lunenburg's Methodists laid the cornerstone for their new church. When completed two years later, it became the largest in the town and at that time had the largest congregation, gained largely through revivals.

Roman Catholics built their St. Norbert's chapel in 1840 and the Baptists had their own church by 1884.

Schools

Until the passage of the Free School Act in 1864 parents had to pay for most of their children's education.

Lunenburg ratepayers met shortly after the Act became law and voted unanimously to build and support an academy on the Parade. The frame raising of a one-storey building the following year called for a royal salute by the Volunteer Artillery Company from Blockhouse Hill. When this building burnt in 1893, there was much discussion about moving the site for a new structure to Gallows Hill. In the end Lunenburg got the finest school building in the province on a most spectacular site. A classic Victorian design, with a sweeping prospect of the town and harbour, it remains a landmark. In one of the four large corner towers was hung the school bell, weighing over 600 pounds. Presentation of prizes for student excellence was always a much attended occasion. There had been no few 'wiseacres' who prophesied that it would never be filled, when they learned of the large size for the planned assembly hall. For the students' Christmas 1913 entertainment, which included musical performances and recitations, as well as physical drills by the Grade IX girls, the crowd not only filled the hall to capacity, but overflowed into the aisles and hallways.

*A typical Lunenburg parlour in the late 19th century.
Note the number of pictures, pieces of china and
furniture. The lady is likely a member of the Bailly family
as a member of that family took this picture. Earlier in
the century this room would have been sparsely furnished.
Below: A Christmas tree in the same parlour. Right: the
75th Regimental Band with J.T. Arenburg, Conductor*

Music

In his essay on the town's history, Harry Hewitt
declared that "The Grand Opera of New York I
matched with the accomplishments of the native sons
and daughters of Lunenburg, their music glorious in
its simplicity and naturalness as opposed to the more
grand and artificial music of the Metropolitan
[Opera]." Hewitt was writing of the glorious music

tradition that the original
settlers brought with them, and
more than any other aspect of their
culture, passed on to succeeding
generations. Hymn singing and
church choirs from the earliest days
gave spiritual and musical voice to
this wonderful inheritance.

Christmas Eve and Christmas
Day services in Lunenburg churches
were filled with sacred music and
must have been a transcendental

experience for many worshippers. The music was never
more magnificent than for Christmas 1912. At the
Methodist Church W.A. Whynacht directed the choir in a
Christmas cantata, "The Adoration." This performance
drew from a critic the comment that it was "one of the
most cleverly rendered musical numbers ever given in
Lunenburg." The Presbyterians had the opportunity of
hearing "The Oratorio-Cantata" under the direction of
Allan Morash and 12 soloists. A "splendid success" was
how the *Progress-Enterprise* reported on the performance
by choir and soloists at Zion Lutheran. The young people
of St. John's continued the tradition begun in the 1830s of
decorating the church for Christmas and other festivals.
Evergreen wreaths extended along the pillars and were
suspended from the rafters. A cross hung from the
chancel arch ablaze with electric lights. For the Sunday
evening after Christmas, there was a full choral service
with soloists under the direction of organist and
choirmaster, M. Penn Spicer. John Arenburg's rendering
of Sole Nevin's the "Rosary" was moving and compelling.

Many of those who performed
and directed sacred music gave freely of their talents for
concerts and benefits. These took place in church
basements, the Drill Shed and the Temperance Hall.

Lunenburg became renowned for its bands. The first
band dates from the late 1830s, known as The Artillery
Band; it may have first performed during the town's
celebrations for Queen Victoria's coronation in 1837. This
band had two successors before the formation of the 75th

Volunteers Battalion Band. First under William Delaney and then John Arenburg, the band performed on every civic occasion. A typical musical entertainment, held at the Drill Hall in 1901, provided audiences with marches, overtures, solos, and waltzes. During the playing of "Il Travatore", the lights were turned off, enhancing the beauty of the number.

As the result of their outstanding musicianship at the 1909 Dominion Exhibition in Halifax, the band was selected to play at the Boston Mechanics Exhibition. There, a critic who had heard all the best bands for years at the Exhibition and also the Coldstream Guards and the Black Watch, supposed to be the finest in the World, declared he "had never heard any band to produce the music that took such a hold on the people as the 75th Regiment Band of Lunenburg, Nova Scotia."

the three-mile race and the Maritime provinces' record for the five-mile. The town soon had Nova Scotia's finest bicycle race track.

Rupert Kaulbach introduced organized hockey in 1898 when teams from Lunenburg and Bridgewater competed for the first time. He had learned hockey while attending Upper Canadian colleges. For many years the players wore no padding whatsoever; the seven-man teams—a goalkeeper, two defencemen, a centre, a rover, and left and right wingmen—played a full game of two 30-minute periods. Substitution was allowed only if there was a serious injury. In the 1908 season the Lunenburg Victorias, in blue and white uniforms, went through the whole season without a losing a game on home ice. During one week they played five away games against teams in Kentville, Wolfville, Windsor, and Halifax without a single loss.

Sports

Towards the end of the century, the young men and women of Lunenburg entered enthusiastically into the growing sports movement. They established a YMCA in 1890 and then formed the Lunenburg Amateur Athletic Association. This association sponsored the 1896 Lunenburg Bicycle Race. Thomas Naas broke the provincial record in

These eight players in their red and white uniforms formed the first Lunenburg Falcons Hockey Team in 1930. Back Row, left to right: Bert Corkum, Jim Knickle and Spike Walters. Middle Row, left to right: Rae Schwartz and Victor Corkum. Front Row, left to right: Charlie Nauss, Clyde Schwartz and Bill Mossman. Inset: The King Brothers High Wire Bicycle Team. Billy King is centre.

A KISS FROM LUNENBURG

578-2

The team had two of the finest hockey players ever produced in Lunenburg, Fred Fox Sr. and Garnet Burns. They and their teammates worked a twelve-hour day before lacing on their skates for a game. In 1912, Lunenburg, Bridgewater, and Liverpool formed the South Shore Hockey League. The season lasted from early January to as late in March as the ice permitted. The Victorias played numerous exhibition games around the western end of the province. Against Yarmouth the Victorias gained a reputation for being "all heavy fellows."

Aside from team sports, winter was a time to skate to band music in the rink, or to go on sleighing trips, finishing with dinner at such popular establishments as the King's Hotel. In the summer there were yacht races and regattas, picnics and excursions to such places as Chester for the annual canoe, boat, and swimming races. Motorboats, decorated with flags, their occupants in holiday attire would depart in a flotilla. In 1913, J.C. Rockwell's motorboat (he was the manager of Lunenburg

GOLDWASHING NEAR LUNENBURG.

VIEW OF LUNENBURG FROM BATTERY POINT.—SEE SUPPLEMENT, PAGE 352.

Foundry) defeated the American *Hackmatack*, a 20-knot racer, over a three-mile course. This victory spoke well for the Lunenburg Foundry's engines.

As the town confidently entered the new century, a visitor describing Lunenburg for Halifax newspaper readers wrote that the town presents an "attractive appearance from every approach, whether by land or water:"

"Its handsome buildings, substantial residences, surrounding hills dotted with well-tilled farms, its fleet of vessels and boats at anchor in the bay present to the eye a panorama of scenic beauty such as is not afforded by any other town in the south shore of Nova Scotia. Everywhere the commercial interest of the people is apparent. Large and substantial warehouses

LUNENBURG BAND STAND AND COURT HOUSE, LUNENBURG, N.S.

Harlan Brown painted this lovely view of Lunenburg Harbour around 1905.

and wharves line the waterfront almost the entire length of the town, where every year is landed and stored the harvest of the sea (amounting to upwards of one million dollars in value), gathered by the strong arms of thousands of hardy fishermen, whose fleet of clipper fishing craft number one for every day of the year. Besides these wharves and warehouses, there are many large retail stores whose plate-glass fronts and immense stocks [are] evidence of the enterprise and solidity of the business men and the affluence of its citizens."

On July 1, 1914, the *Progress-Enterprise* carried an advertisement for Lunenburgers to see for the first time at the Music Hall "the genuine Edison Talking Pictures."

They were assured these were not simply moving pictures, but "laughing, talking and singing figures."

A month later, Europe plunged into four long years of war. The *Progress-Enterprises* headline on August 9, 1914, read "The Peace of the World Disturbed."

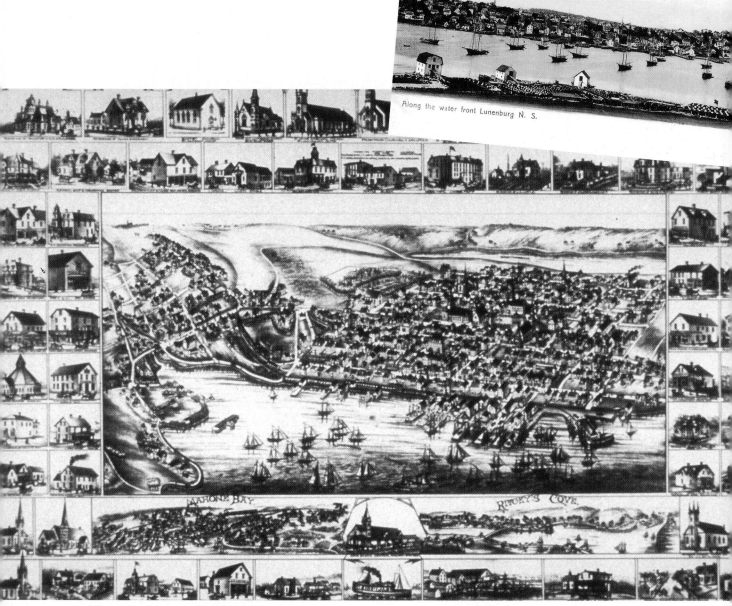

A bird's-eye view of prospering Lunenburg in 1879. Note how New Town has grown in less than two decades. Another bird's-eye view was published in 1890, but the publishers reused the 1879 plate with no changes to the Old Town buildings and wharves.

Chapter 3

1914-1945

I n the nineteenth century the people of Lunenburg experienced the peace and security that came with membership in the British Empire at its zenith. In the first half of the twentieth century they lived through two world wars and the Great Depression. Two generations of youth answered the call to the colours, while on the home front her citizens threw their energies into the war effort. The fishing industry underwent far more revolutionary change than in the whole of the previous 100 years. For those who lived through those times, however, their most vivid memories remain the racing victories of the famous schooner *Bluenose*.

The First World War

Within weeks of the outbreak of war in 1914, the Department of Militia and Defence called on the 75th Lunenburg Regiment to provide a company for a composite battalion to garrison the Halifax Citadel. Soon Lunenburgers were training in "mimic warfare" on Camp Hill. But Sir Sam Hughes, the wilful Minister of the Militia, decided to discard the carefully prepared mobilization plan for calling up the 75th and other volunteer militia units across the nation. Instead, he substituted his own scheme of raising men directly and putting them into numbered infantry battalions. Young Canadians, swept up with an extraordinary show of patriotic fervour for King and Country, volunteered in large numbers. A Canadian Expeditionary Force of 32,000 men sailed in October 1914 for Britain. Their baptism in battle came in

April 1915 at Ypres when the Germans attacked using poison gas; in four days of heroism and sacrifice they suffered over 6,000 casualties in repelling the enemy assault.

Among those Canadians of the First Contingent, were an "able little band" of Lunenburgers, including Charlie Cossman and Ned Coldwell; both were to see the war through. Major province-wide recruiting began in October for the 25th Battalion, the first wholly Nova Scotian unit to go into battle. Four officers of the 75th enlisted—Captains J.W. Margeson and W.L. Whitford and Lieutenants C.M. Mosher and V.P. Murphy. Among the other ranks from the 75th joining the colours were Sergeants Roy King and Hector Boliver, Assistant Quartermaster Harry MacIntosh, and Privates Joseph Boliver and J. Nelson. Roy King was to go through the whole war, be badly wounded and return to the

Jesson Zinck probably posed for this photograph before going overseas in the First World War.

The Band of Nova Scotia's 85th Battalion. Jesson Zinck is in the back row and third from left. Below: An 85th Battalion cook tent.

front, but to die in an English hospital within months of the war's end; his elder brother Ronald also served in the trenches, only to die a short time before Roy. They were the only sons of Harry King and his wife.

The *Progress-Enterprise* called on those who did not offer to serve to do "all things necessary to keep Lunenburg's position as a component part of the British Empire where it should be." The ladies of Lunenburg formed a Red Cross Auxiliary, the Boscawen Chapter of the Imperial Daughters of the Empire (I.O.D.E.) and a Women's Institute. They were behind the work within the town and county for the Canadian Patriotic Fund, formed to raise money to care for the wives and children of soldiers overseas. They began their efforts in November 1914 with the first of many patriotic concerts at the Opera House. They also raised money for ambulances and field kitchens.

Their most beneficial and sustained endeavour was providing surgical supplies and clothing. The Red Cross Auxiliary made, collected, packed and shipped bales of such articles as surgical shirts, socks, mittens, pyjama suits, towels, dressings of all types, and bandages. Inside the socks they put little notes to the soldiers. One soldier, after experiencing the Ypres battle, wrote to Mrs. Amram Hebb thanking her for a pair of socks: "We had not had our boots off for six days, so you can judge how we all felt to

get our feet washed and a pair of good new socks on." The Militia Department issued instructions to Canadian women on how to knit military socks; the regulations took up a full column and a half in the *Progress-Enterprise*! Between June 1915 and the following June, the Red Cross packed and sent off 7,155 pieces of work, including 859 pairs of socks and 3,096 bandages; as well, they shipped such necessaries as toothpaste and brushes, antiseptic powder, writing paper and bootlaces.

Letters became the chief means that townspeople could learn of their kin in the trenches. Ned Coldwell, one of the "Bull's Eye" men of the 75th, described how he and his friends survived in the trenches; he reported that none of the Lunenburg boys had as yet been killed, though some had been wounded. Bernard Smith wrote his sister: "I have not been in a real bed for six months, or my trousers off for about the same time ... When we hear a shell coming, we dive for the dug-out and yell back to Fritzie for he is bum shot." Captain J.W. Margeson wrote to the editor of the *Progress-Enterprise* reporting on many in the 25th Battalion. Mrs A.J. MacDonald passed on

The War Memorial, Lunenburg, Nova Scotia.—9.

letters for publication from her sister, S.C. Robley, a nursing sister at the No. 2 Canadian Hospital in France.

From the summer of 1915 the dreaded telegrams began to arrive. Among those killed was Captain O.G. Dauphinee. Corporal Bergu Emiel Olsen, a Norwegian who had come to Lunenburg some ten years before, became the town's first decorated soldier when, with "great gallantry and resource," he repaired telephone wires under heavy shell fire. Later he was badly wounded at Ypres and became the first to return home. In December 1916 Lieutenant Henry

Greenwood of Lunenburg received the Military Cross for "conspicuous gallantry."

After the recruitment of the 25th, came the call for volunteers to fill up the ranks of the 85th, the parent unit of the Nova Scotia Highland Brigade. Hundreds lined the streets from the Drill Hall to the railway station to bid farewell to the town's volunteers as they marched to board a train for their journey to France. The Boscawen Chapter of the I.O.D.E. gave each soldier a box lunch for the ride to Halifax.

In its end-of-year editorial for 1915, the *Progress-Enterprise* wrote confidently that the result was not in doubt and the war would be over shortly; the editor's major concern was the number of "footloose" young men there might then be around. Within a month of such ill-fated optimism, the government called for an army of 500,000 with Nova Scotia's share being 30,000 men. Halifax and the western counties were called upon to fill up the ranks of another battalion, the 219th. Colonel Allison Borden began his recruiting campaign in Lunenburg with a big rally on February 26, 1916 and ended at Wolfville on March 12.

The 219th was broken up, however, in England to become reinforcements for the 25th and the 85th. Most from Lunenburg were to serve in these two famous Nova Scotian battalions. One of the last of the 85th to die was Lieutenant Eric Hamilton, leading his men in the capture of German strong point; a tablet in St. John's Church remembers his self-sacrifice. Those in the 85th at the war's end took part in the Great March of Triumph on May 3, 1919, through London.

In June the first group of soldiers arrived back. A month later the town celebrated a Peace Day, beginning

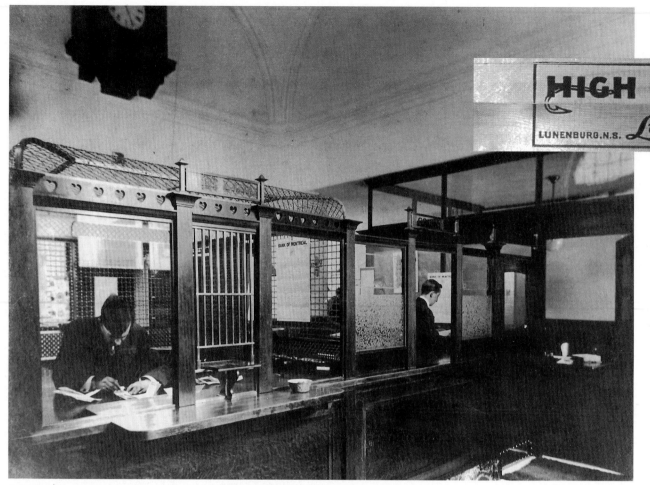

Interior of the Bank of Montreal at 12 King Street, c. 1930

with a royal salute, church services in the morning, and in the afternoon, a baseball match between Lunenburg and Liverpool veterans. A week later came what the *Progress-Enterprise* called, "the most popular function ever held in Lunenburg" when the men were the town's guests at a banquet in the beautiful room of the Oddfellows' Hall. Mayor William Duff proposed the toast to the honoured guests, while the Reverend Captain A.J. MacDonald, who had temporarily left St. Andrew's to serve, replied on behalf of the veterans. Mrs James Hirtle, in speaking for I.O.D.E., made one of the "most eloquent and perfect speeches heard," before calling out the names of the returned soldiers. Each of the over 200 present

received a pair of cuff links from the Boscawen Chapter and a Certificate of Recognition from the town.

From a Salt to a Fresh Fishery

The veterans returned to a Lunenburg that in 1918 had experienced its most profitable year in the fishing and shipbuilding industries. With no European competition in traditional markets, Lunenburg fish sold for unprecedented prices. Fishermen reported that never in the industry's history had the Grand Banks so teemed with fish.

This success came in spite of the sinking of nine fishing

vessels by German submarines in the last months of the war. The last ship to be sunk was the *Elsie Porter* with her 22-man crew, 150 miles off St. John's, Newfoundland. After

the submarine fired two shots across her bow the crew took to their dories. Captain Irwin Eisenhauer was the last to leave the vessel, but not before he followed the old tradition of sea and kissed the railing. After questioning Captain Eisenhauer, the U-boat captain let them go. It took them five days of sailing in open dories before they sighted St. John's harbour. Almost immediately after the war ended, however, the salt fishery faced serious challenges from renewed European competition, the introduction of trawlers and especially the growth of the fresh fish market. Many Lunenburg fishermen opposed the introduction of trawlers and onshore freezing to preserve catches because of the fewer number of fishermen needed compared to the traditional salt fishery. Saltfish exporters like the W.C. Smith and Company, founded by William Smith in 1899 as a small fish outfitting and supply business, were still making money. By the mid-1920s the family-managed firm of W.C. Smith had grown into the largest saltfish exporter on Canada's east coast, but its board of directors recognized that the future lay in the frozen fish business.

A public meeting began the process leading to the opening in 1926 of a fish processing plant with cold storage facilities. The plant was owned by the newly formed Lunenburg Sea Products, a subsidiary of W.C. Smith and Company. But there was so little local enthusiasm for this venture that the Smith family had to buy up most of the bond issue to pay for the $80,000 plant. In an innovative move, the company also introduced the recently discovered technique of filleting, which much improved the marketing of fresh and frozen products.

Such barrels as these were used to ship fish to the West Indian and South American markets. The boots are typical of those worn by fishermen in the 19th and 20th centuries

The introduction of steam trawlers in the 1920s meant that instead of catching fish by baited hooks, whether by handlining or trawling lines, large quantities of fish were taken by dragging nets across the ocean bottom. By 1930, when the catches using the traditional schooner and dory technology fell to disastrous levels at the same time that prices collapsed in a deepening depression, there was a call for the complete abolition of trawlers. However, European and American fishermen were using them and 100 foreign trawlers were operating off the east coast. Lunenburg had to follow.

Off Rum Row

In 1920 the United States enacted legislation to prohibit the legal sale of alcohol. This disastrous social experiment lasted for the next 13 years. Massive

Top: Crew of the Bluenose with Captain Angus Walters in centre with pipe. Left: Crew of the schooner Alcala taken in the 1920s

smuggling resulted, which made hypocrites of most and corrupted many. Of Canada's East Coast seafaring and fishing communities, Lunenburg had the most experienced captains and crews to enagage in the business of rum running. Although the rewards could be great, so were the risks. Initially, Nova Scotian fishing schooners, known as "blacks" to the American Coast Guard, brought liquor directly from Europe to points close to the American coast for pick up under darkness by small, fast shore-based vessels. For the transshipment of liquor to be smuggled into the United States, a huge infrastructure with warehouses soon arose on the small French island of St. Pierre, off Newfoundland. Vessels involved in the smuggling gathered especially off Long Island, New Jersey and Boston, which became known as "Rum Row." With the bank fishery declining, schooner owners sold or chartered their vessels to organized crime syndicates. Captains and crews were found to sail them. As Lunenburg's temperance advocates recognized, there was more money in rum running than in fishing. A "conspiracy of silence" descended, broken only occasionally, such as when a number of wives who were workers in the temperance cause went public in 1924 on the refusal of their husbands to get out of the business.

Well over a hundred vessels, many of them from the town or manned by Lunenburgers, lay off Rum Row at any one time. Before Christmas the traffic became particularly heavy; in December 1924 the *Argus* reported that the Lunenburg schooners *Arcvola, Auragania,* the *Ida* and the *Grace* were seen on Rum Row off loading quantities of liquor from a British steamer. Sometimes, as in the case of the Lunenburg tern schooner the *Vincent A. White* in January 1924, the vessel and her complete cargo of liquor would be sold on the high seas.

It took a tragedy such as the fate of the *Beryl M. Corkum* to illuminate the workings of the rum trade. Rafuse and Sons of Conquerall Bank built the *Corkum* in 1914 and she worked the freighting trades until her owners, entirely Lunenburg people, had their agents, the Lunenburg Outfitting Company, put her into rum running without carrying any insurance on her. She became one of the vessels plying the liquor trade from Bridgetown, Barbados to Halifax and St. Pierre, disposing of her cargoes on the New England coast en route. Her owners changed her registry from Lunenburg to Bridgetown. On May 25, 1924, she cleared from Halifax with 4,000 cases of liquor under charter to American interests. She disposed of her cargo off Rum Row and was

supposed to have left there just before a terrif August storm hit the coast. In late September two American fishing schooners brought word to Boston that they had sighted the *Corkum* capsized and derelict off Georges Bank with no sign of her captain, William Zwicker, and her five-man crew, all except one from Lunenburg County.

Hugh H. Corkum of Lunenburg in his book *On Both Sides of the Law* vividly describes the rum running trade. In 1928 he took ship as an able seaman with the *Harbour Trader,* a rum runner completely disguised as an ocean tug; her crew were all respectable family men who were simply doing a job that gave them a living at a time when the fishery and freighting were depressed. They made big money for the depression years; a crewman was paid $75 a month and given $150 bonus for every successful trip to Rum Row. Usually the *Harbour Trader* made monthly trips. The crew were never told of the agreed arrangements for off loading.

The *Harbour Trader* went first to St. Pierre where she loaded up with all brands of whisky, liquors of other kinds and the better brands of French champagne. She then proceeded along the Nova Scotian coast before departing for the American coast, where she would stay well offshore to keep away from Coast Guard cutters. After receiving radio messages with the arrangements for the "drop," the *Harbour Trader* would sail up to the

Chief of Police Hugh H. Corkum taken in the 1945 (and keys)

twelve-mile limit under darkness. Sometimes a cluster of fast open-deck motor boats met them close to shore; other times the captain took the vessel right into New York harbour before off-loading her cargo. After over a decade at sea, Hugh Corkum decided he had had enough. He joined the Lunenburg town police force. In 1941 he became Police Chief, a position he held with great merit until he retired in 1976.

Rum running, however, became an increasingly dangerous occupation as the Americans put destroyers and other armed ships into the battle against smuggling. In reply, the smugglers built special purpose high-powered rum runners, painted grey, that sailed low in the water and looked like submarines or, as some called them, "banana" boats. Probably around a dozen were Lunenburg built. It was in one such vessel, the *Josephine K*, that Captain William Cluett met his death in January 1931 when an American coast guard cutter off Rum Row deliberately fired a shell into her. Hundreds attended his funeral service at St. John's Church. In a forceful sermon the Reverend W.E. Ryder called the act nothing less than murder. Such incidents he charged were becoming a daily occurrence, "inevitable tragedies that follow from the hypocrisy of prohibition."

The Fastest Fishing Schooner in the North Atlantic

In the inter-war years the story of the fabled Lunenburg schooner the *Bluenose* embodied the town's spirit. As the era of schooner fishing was coming to an end, the *Bluenose's* racing triumphs became a source of enormous pride to Lunenburgers—and indeed to all Canadians. In Lunenburg's history there had never been a moment of greater excited anticipation than on March 26, 1921. The town's entire population descended on Smith and Rhuland's shipyard. Hundreds of gaily-bedecked craft plied to and fro. At ten o'clock the *Bluenose* slid gracefully into the harbour. A schooner, the *Halifax*

Herald told its readers, of "surpassing beauty and one in which the aspirations of the Dominion are worthily embodied." Her captain, Angus Walters, believed he had a schooner fast enough to take back from Gloucester, Massachusetts the

International Fisherman's Trophy for the fastest schooner in the North Atlantic.

The trophy had grown out of the 1920 America's Cup race in which the British yacht *Shamrock IV* challenged and lost to the American defender, the *Resolute*. What particularly intrigued and astonished Lunenburg and Gloucester fishermen was that one race had to be postponed because the winds had increased to 23 knots. These men, used to sailing in strong winds, believed they could put on a much better show than the expensive yachts built for the America's Cup. The resulting controversy engendered such intense speculation that Senator William H. Dennis, proprietor of the *Halifax Herald*, put up a trophy for an international schooner race with a cash prize of $3,000.

Nine Lunenburg schooners competed off Halifax Harbour in October 1920 to determine which should face the winner of the American elimination series. It was a close contest between the *Delawana* and the *Gilbert Walters*, whose captain was Angus Walters. The

Delawana won over the 45-mile course by five minutes. But the *Delawana* couldn't handle the Gloucester winner of the American elimination series, the *Esperanto*, in the first International Schooner Race off Halifax Harbour later that month.

No one felt the loss to the Americans more keenly than did Angus Walters. He and the Smith and Rhuland yard reached an agreement to build a vessel to bring the trophy back to Canada. In Halifax, an unassuming and unknown self-taught marine architect, William James Roue, was

Above left: Wallace MacAskill took this wonderful photograph of Captain Angus Walters with the International Fishermen's Trophy. Above right: Bluenose crew with their trophies. Above: The Bluenose in 1931

then earning his living as manager of the family firm, Roue's Carbonated Waters Ltd. Although he had never before designed a fishing schooner, Walters and the yard accepted Roue's as the best sail and hull designs. The building of the 121st schooner by Smith and Rhuland began in December. The Governor General, the Duke of Devonshire, came to drive the first bolt into the timbers of the *Bluenose's* keel. As work continued over the winter months, spectators gathered daily, sometimes by the hundreds, to watch and to comment. The consensus of opinion became that she had "the finest shaped underbody of any vessel ever turned out" by Smith and Rhuland.

After her launching the *Bluenose* sailed to the banks for a season of fishing, for her owners meant her to earn her keep. In October the *Bluenose* took on eight other Lunenburg salt-bankers, easily coming out the winner in the elimination round. On the American side, the *Esperanto* had sunk off Sable Island; the *Elsie* replaced her.

The Bluenose racing against the Henry Ford in 1922. The Bluenose showed her fine sailing qualities in this race. Henry Ford could not stay the course when it blew hard.

Off Halifax Harbour in October 1921, the *Bluenose* defeated the *Elsie* in two races. In the first she crossed the finish line 13 minutes ahead; in the second she led across the line by more than three miles. In the following year the *Bluenose* and her challenger, the *Henry Ford*, raced off Boston. With the winds exceeding 25 knots, the Bluenose again demonstrated her fine sailing qualities; the *Henry Ford* could not stay the course when it blew hard.

The Americans next built the *Columbia*. The 1923 race would be in Canadian waters. On October 29, 1923, the first race took place. While heading back into Halifax Harbour, the *Columbia* forced the *Bluenose* close to shallow water, but as was her right the *Bluenose* held her course; she hooked a bight of a jib downhaul rope of the *Columbia* and pulled her a short distance before the rope broke. As the *Bluenose* was to the windward she sailed away to cross the line first.

The second race proved even more controversial. Although the *Bluenose* led all the way, the *Columbia* protested on a buoy technicality. The Race Committee awarded the race to the *Columbia*. Angus Walters felt the *Bluenose* had won and both he and the American captain said that they would race again. The committee refused to recognize another race. Lunenburg kept the trophy by default and received half the prize money. There was so much sour feeling generated that it was another eight years before *Bluenose* competed again for the International Fisherman's Trophy.

Meanwhile the *Bluenose* continued her life as a salt-banker. Boston racing enthusiasts, however, were determined to win the International Trophy and built a new challenger, the *Gertrude L. Thebaud*. In 1931 the *Bluenose* and the *Thebaud* met off Halifax Harbour. The *Bluenose* easily outclassed her challenger, removing any doubt which was the faster. Not until 1938 did the *Bluenose* race again in an international series. She was 17 years old and weather weary. In a series of five races, the *Bluenose* defeated once more the *Thebaud* to retain

Above: A Wallace MacAskill photo of the Bluenose in full sail

her racing supremacy. But she never raced again. She came to an ignoble end in 1946 on a Haitian reef.

Community Life in Hard Times

The *Bluenose's* racing triumphs served to keep spirits up in the face the hardest times any Lunenburg generation had known. Throughout the Depression the churches remained vital centres of social and religious life. The great festivals of Christmas and Easter continued to be celebrated with magnificent music and the church interiors beautifully decorated; at Christmas there was greenery and at Easter the altars were decked with lilies and white hyacinths.

As well as sacred music, Lunenburgers could hear local performances of Gilbert and Sullivan operettas, the Lunenburg Mixed Quartet, which also performed on radio, a 40-voice mixed choir, and the Lunenburg Male Choir whose repertoire ranged from minstrel shows to Handel's Messiah. In 1939 the choir went to the New York World Fair where they participated in a grand concert broadcast over the Columbia and Mutual Radio Networks. The Lunenburg Academy had its Beethoven Choral Club. If any single person made all this music happen, it was Mrs. B.G. Oxner, a contralto and choir director; she was one of 24 Canadians who represented their country in the Westminster Abbey Choir for George VI's coronation in 1937.

During these hard times the town was usually able to ice a fairly strong hockey team, the Victorias, who were renamed in 1930 as the Falcons with red and white as their colours. Natural ice made for a short season and not until 1928 did Lunenburg even have a good indoor rink. When interest in the game seemed to falter, Rupert Kaulbach came to the rescue. He saw no reason why if the *Bluenose* put Nova Scotia on the "Racing Map," why Lunenburg could not be on the province's "Hockey Map."

In 1931 the Falcons had one their best seasons, and under coach Jimmie Foley won the South Shore League. They went on to defeat the Wolfville Cohorts and the Digby Ravens to reach the finals for the Nova Scotia

Senior title against the Truro Bearcats. The Bearcats were undefeated, so the Falcons did well to win one game before the Truro team took the title; the Bearcats went on to take the Maritime title and only just lost out in the Eastern Canadian finals against the Hamilton Tigers.

Generally, Lunenburg had little trouble winning the South Shore League. In the senior playoffs the Falcons defeated Annapolis by scores of 6-2 and 8-2, but went down to defeat before the powerful Kentville Wildcats. Before the following season opened, the Falcons lost such star players as Fred Fox Jr. to other teams and Bridgewater took the South Shore League title. Although for the 1937 season Fred Fox Jr. returned, he and two other players were out for the season

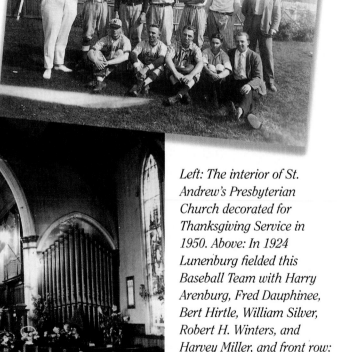

Left: The interior of St. Andrew's Presbyterian Church decorated for Thanksgiving Service in 1950. Above: In 1924 Lunenburg fielded this Baseball Team with Harry Arenburg, Fred Dauphinee, Bert Hirtle, William Silver, Robert H. Winters, and Harvey Miller, and front row: Ray Schwartz, Joe Boliver, Hector Boliver, Murray Silver, and Billy Boliver.

because of a car accident in which a third player was killed. Bridgewater again took the league title. This was the last year for senior hockey on the South Shore; not until 1952 would the Falcons again play senior hockey.

The first Fishermen's Picnic was held in 1916 and this autumn event continued until 1929 when it became Nova Scotia's first and only Fisheries Exhibition. It drew thousands from all over to watch parades, races of every description on land and water, band concerts and to dine from endless tables of food. Upwards of 11,000 attended the three-day 1931 Exhibition. For its employees and their families, the Lunenburg Foundry held an annual picnic at Lakeside, the beautiful summer home of the president, J.J. Kinley.

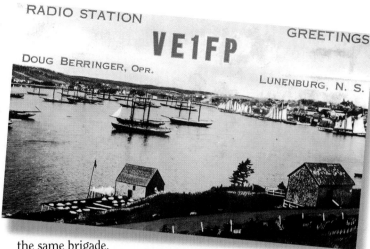

RADIO STATION
VE1FP
GREETINGS
DOUG BERRINGER, OPR.
LUNENBURG, N. S.

The Second World War

By the late 1930s the worst of the Great Depression was over, but the clouds of war were hovering again. It would take six long years to destroy Hitler and Nazism. Lunenburgers once again heeded the call of King and Country. On September 1, 1939, Lieutenant Colonel G.W. Bullock (in civilian life the rector of Bridgewater's Holy Trinity Church) received the order to mobilize the West Nova Scotia Regiment. There had been changes in military organization during the inter-war years, but when the call came there was a militia ready for service.

In 1922 the old 69th and 75th Volunteer Battalions had been redesignated as the Annapolis and Lunenburg Regiments. In the early 1930s Captain W.P. Potter, adjutant of the Lunenburg Regiment, designed a new badge for his regiment. His design consisted of a shield superimposed on a maple leaf, and containing in relief a replica of an original blockhouse built to defend the early settlement and of the *Bluenose*. Beneath this design he placed the regimental motto *"Semper Fidelis."*

Before the First World War, the 69th and 75th had carried out their annual training together at Camp Aldershot near Kentville. After the war the Lunenburg and Annapolis Regiments continued to train there as part of

the same brigade.

In 1936 The West Nova Scotia Regiment was created by amalgamating the Lunenburg and Annapolis Regiments. Two of the four rifle companies were on the South Shore, with "A" Company in Lunenburg and Headquarters Company at Bridgewater. The West Novas' new badge consisted of a crown and a shield superimposed upon an eight-pointed sunburst representing the dawn, as Nova Scotia was then Canada's most easterly province. Incorporated into the design were Saint Andrew's Cross from the province's flag, the Mayflower as Nova Scotia's floral emblem, and replicas of the Acadian Chapel at Grand Pré and the *Bluenose*.

Lieutenant Beck, the Lunenburg Regiment bandmaster, adapted the regimental march "Wenosco" for his new regiment. The West Novas perpetuated the Lunenburg Regiment's motto *"Semper Fidelis."*

On Colonel Bullock's order to mobilize, "A" Company in Lunenburg reported 55 men ready for duty under the command of Major O.B. Berringer. Once mobilized, the whole regiment took over temporarily the Lunenburg County Exhibition Grounds in Bridgewater before going to Aldershot to begin serious training. By early 1940 the regiment was engaged in training in England. On July 10, 1943, the West Novas landed on a Sicilian beach, the first of many battles in the Italian Campaign.

Once again, Lunenburg's war effort saw the local Red Cross Auxiliary and the I.O.D.E. in the forefront. Both organizations were soon busy fund-raising and sending off such knitted

In July 1942 these members of the Lunenburg Girls' Volunteer Service Corps posed outside Zion Lutheran Church in their natty new uniforms. The uniforms combined khaki skirtwaists, navy skirts and tams, the latter having embrodiered emblems in gold on the side front. Front row, left to right: Corporal Frances Silver, Corporal Katherine Riser, Lance Corporal Beatrice Stoddart, Lieutenant Ethel Naus, Lieutenant Dorothy Creuse, Major Marguerite Schwartz (Officer Commanding), Captain Joyce Smith (Adjutant), Lieutenant Isobel Spindler, Sergeant Major Flora Tanner, Sergeant Peggy Miller, Sergeant Frances Geldert. Second row, left to right: Phyllis McLellan, Dorothy Anderson, Golda Brenton, Lance Corporal Christine Hall, Lance Corporal Margaret Oxner, Lance Corporal Theresa Mason, Iris Oxner, Rita Tobin, Annie (unknown). Third row, left to right: Christine Iversen, Greta Colp, Erna Tanner, Marie Young, Harriet Deal, Betty McIsaac, Isabel Butt. Standing at rear: Supervising Officer, D.J. Bourque.

items as balaclava caps and minesweeper jackets. Navy League women made hundreds of ditty bags for merchant navy sailors. R.M. Whynacht became head of the war saving campaign. In seven Victory Loan Campaigns, the town led the county and surpassed its objective. The Fire Department and the Canadian Legion combined to host fund-raising garden parties; at the 1941 party the star attraction was a demonstration by a Canadian Women's Army Corps precision drill squad of "khaki-clad girls in their smart uniforms," a sight not seen in the First World War. On numerous occasions, Lunenburg musicians travelled to perform at Camp Aldershot, the major training centre in the Maritimes. Citizens formed Air Raid Protection squads, emergency hospitals were designated, and black-outs were practised against possible German air raids or naval shelling. At the first of many blood donor clinics over 1,000 turned out.

After the 1940 German conquest of Norway, 600 Norwegians who had been hunting whales in the Antarctic Ocean arrived at Halifax. Lunenburg offered them a wartime home and Camp Norway came into being. The Norwegian Navy turned the camp into a naval training station and the Norwegian Army also used it for training. Zion Lutheran became the Norwegians' church. They gathered there especially to celebrate on the eve of the Sankt Hans Aften—Norway's mid-summer festival of the Feast of St. John the Baptist. The town received its first royal visit when Norway's Crown Prince Olav and Crown Princess Martha visited the camp in 1941 and again the following year. When the Norwegian Navy decided to move the training establishment to the United States, the Royal Canadian Navy took the camp over to house sailors in port awaiting the refitting of their ships.

The Lunenburg Foundry refitted over 100 corvettes, minesweepers and frigates as well as manufacturing equipment for new vessels. From making stoves, furnaces and marine engines employing a hundred men, the foundry grew to a payroll of more than 500, including a key group of Norwegian engineers. Over 100 foundry

employees enlisted in the Armed Forces.

To meet war demands the fishery expanded making 1940 returns the best for a decade. Smith and Rhuland launched its largest schooner ever, the *Sherman Zwicker*, in March 1942. But the contract to build two R.C.A.F. marine rescue craft proved just how seaworthy were vessels built by the yard. The British Ministry of Transport contracted for two TANAC 99 tugs; these became the 199th and 200th vessels launched by the yard, an event that attracted hundreds of spectators.

By late 1941, 148 people of the town had enlisted in the Armed Forces; in the 1942 plebiscite, the town voted five to one for conscription. In early 1942 a U-boat torpedoed Warren Allen's merchant vessel, making him the town's first casualty to enemy action. Captain Edward Jensen also died after a U-boat attack on the barquetine *Angelus,* heading for Halifax with a West Indian cargo. Fred Fox Jr.,

Crew of H.M.C.S. Lunenburg

an outstanding athlete who joined the R.C.A.F., was shot down over Italy and became a prisoner-of-war. By the autumn of 1943, with the West Novas battling their way up the Italian mainland, Lunenburg received its first casualty reports of serving townsmen; Privates Roy Arthur Young and Harry Schnare were reported as killed in action and among the seriously wounded were Morton Allen, brother of Warren, Lieutenant William Himmelman for the second time and Captain Harry Eisenhauer. Winning the Military Medal, Private "Jackie" King was first from the town to be decorated.

In June 1941 on the invitation of Davie Shipyards at Quebec, Mayor A.W. Schwartz attended the launching of H.M.C.S. *Lunenburg*, one the many corvettes coming off the slipways to make up Canada's growing corvette navy. After her commissioning on December 4, she did escort duty from Halifax to St. John's. For her first Christmas the Lunenburg I.O.D.E. chapter sent parcels to the crew. In September 1942 she began a four-month stint escorting convoys between the United Kingdom and Mediterranean for Operation Torch, the allied invasion of North Africa. When this duty finished, she spent a brief time back in Canadian waters before being assigned to escort convoys between the United Kingdom and Gibraltar, as well as patrolling the Northwestern Approaches from her Londonderry, Ireland, base.

In April 1944 the *Lunenburg* went to Portsmouth for D-day invasion duties. For the next five months she was employed primarily in the English Channel. After refitting at Saint John and Halifax, she returned to finish the war in the English Channel. During her service she had four commanders. It was the privilege of the last, Lieutenant Commander W.S. Thompson, to bring her into Lunenburg Harbour shortly after VE Day to be presented with a "Key to the Town." Afterwards, the town gave the crew a banquet. Her end came in 1946 when she was broken up.

As part of the 1st Canadian Division, the West Novas fought their way into the heart of the Italian peninsula at Portenza by September 1943. On the collapse of Mussolini's regime, Hitler threw into the battle for Italy some 25 of the Wehrmacht's finest divisions. A long and bloody struggle ensued. At Ortona in December 1943 the West Novas had their toughest battle so far and their heaviest casualties. Their next major battle was the breaking of the Hitler Line where they particularly distinguished themselves. The spring of 1945 found the regiment in North West Europe for the final battles before the German surrender in May. Major Harry Eisenhauer, who been one the "originals," and had commanded "C" Company from the Hitler Line to the end, brought the regiment home. During its six years of service, the West Novas fought in 21 actions; they left behind 352 killed, while another 1084 were wounded.

Top: Pouring molten steel at Lunenburg Foundry, 1942. Above: The launching of one of the wartime vessels built by Smith and Rhuland. Left: Lunenburg received its first royal visit when Crown Prince Olav and Crown Princess Martha visited Camp Norway in 1941.

Chapter 4

AFTER 1945

hose who served in the Second World War returned to a more confident community than they had left. The war economy had generated a recovery in the fishery and shipbuilding. Although there remained much resistance to the new fishing technology, mid-way through the war, Smith and Rhuland began building vessels that could be converted to dragging trawls across the ocean bottom. In 1945 the newly-formed National Sea Products (resulting from a merger of W.C Smith and

Above: The Cape North was the first of two diesel trawlers ordered by National Sea.

accountant with the old W.C. Smith Company, National Sea grew into a major international company. By 1965 it had 3,500 employees and owned 38 trawlers with another six ordered. A trawler's catch was frozen as soon as it arrived at the processing plant. Although there was consumer resistance to frozen fish, National Sea launched its High Liner frozen fish sticks in the 1950s; this product became the first frozen fish convenience food. The High Liner name became the company's "flagship" consumer brand for the creative mass marketing of fish products.

All this expansion put an enormous strain on the aging 1926 fish processing plant. In 1964 the company opened the largest and most modern fish processing plant in North America. Built at a cost of $8 million, the plant could process "50,000 pounds of fish every hour with a maximum filleting rate of 35,000 to 40,000 pounds an hour and a total annual production capacity of 80 million pounds of raw fish a year." National Sea had

Above and right: On the assembly line at Lunenburg Sea Products in 1941.

Company, its Lunenburg Sea Products and associated companies, with Maritime National Fish in Halifax) ordered two diesel trawlers—the *Cape North* and the *Cape LaHave*.

When the *Cape North* returned from a banks trip on March 21, 1946, the curious and the interested swarmed down to the wharf. They had heard that Captain Napean Crouse reported the *Cape North* had broken the all-time record with a catch of 370,000 pounds of fresh fish; moreover, it had taken her just five and half days. Once again Lunenburg fishermen and entrepreneurs were leading the way forward for the Canadian east coast industry.

The success of the Capes caused National Sea to order steel trawlers. During the 1950s and 1960s under the presidency of C.J. Morrow, who had begun as a young

become the dominant presence in the industry and Lunenburg its centre of operations.

The phenomenal 1950s and 1960s revival of Lunenburg's fishing industry paralleled what her fishermen and merchant class had achieved with the banks fishery a hundred years earlier. It had demonstrated once more the necessity for adopting new fishing technologies and the crucial importance of dynamic local entrepreneurship. The banks fishery gave Lunenburg a half-century of prosperity before trawlers and frozen fresh fish technology brought about another change. In the 1970s massive, indiscriminate over fishing by foreign fishermen, especially the use of factory trawlers by the Soviets and West Germans, caused Canada to establish a 200-mile protective fisheries zone, while giving some preference to Canadian fishermen.

It seemed for a time that Canadian fishing interests could reap an endless harvest with new fishing technologies that permitted year-round operations. In 1985 National Sea overcame fierce opposition from the inshore fishery and introduced factory freezer trawlers. A successor to the original *Cape North*, a new *Cape North* allowed for quick freezing of catches at sea and more efficient processing for higher prices. The fishery seemed set for a bountiful future. However, overexpansion of fishing effort brought the ground fish stocks close to extinction. The closure of the cod fishery in the early 1990s left the industry with an uncertain future.

In meeting the challenge of radical and sudden change in the fishery's prospects, Lunenburg demonstrated once

more her enterprising spirit. A much reduced National Sea survives by concentrating on processing fresh fish caught as far away as the Bering Sea. It is imported in container loads and also directly from foreign freezer trawlers. Lunenburg fishermen still work the lucrative scallop fishery off Georges and Brown banks. Although their mainstay remains serving the fishing industry and ship repair, locally-owned manufacturing enterprises, such as the Lunenburg Foundry and ABCO metal fabricators and machine shop, have continued to find innovative ways to make and market their products. Lunenburg remains pre-eminently a fishing community.

The Second Era of Wooden Sailing Ships

Although the era of schooners, the banks fishery and the triumphs of the *Bluenose* was long past, Lunenburg was able to recapture the flavour of earlier days through the work of building replicas of large sailing vessels. First

Oxen continued to be used for such tasks as hauling coal in the 1950s.

came the project to reconstruct H.M.S. *Bounty*. Although the competition was stiff as any Smith and Rhuland had faced, the yard won the contract to build a replica of the *Bounty* for the Metro-Goldwyn-Mayer (MGM) film "Mutiny on the Bounty." Her construction drew hundreds, just as they had come to watch the *Bluenose* take shape some 40 years earlier. With much fanfare, her 1960 launching demonstrated once again the skill of the yard's shipwrights in building wooden vessels. Most of the crew for the film were Lunenburgers.

Smith and Rhuland's reputation from the *Bounty* was very much the reason that the Americans chose the Lunenburg shipyard to have a H.M.S. *Rose* replica built for their 1976 bicentenary celebrations. The original *Rose*, a 24-gun frigate, was built in Hull, Yorkshire, England in 1756/57. She saw action during the Seven Years War and in the West Indies. As the American Thirteen Colonies moved to outright rebellion, she was first sent to Newport, Rhode Island, to prevent smuggling. Illegal imports had made the port into one of the richest towns in the colonies. The *Rose* proved so successful in reducing smuggling that Rhode Island

H.M.S. Bounty

General Assembly requested the Continental Congress to establish a national navy to deal with her. Congress proceeded to act and established the United States Navy. The British frigate's connection to the founding of the American Navy brought about the building of a replica of the *Rose* for the United States bicentenary.

After further actions during the American War of Independence, the *Rose* came to her end when she was purposefully sunk off Savannah, Georgia, to block the harbour. The action prevented a French invasion fleet from getting close enough to bombard the city, thus the *Rose* saved Savannah

Above: National Sea Products Plant, opened in 1964.
Above right: H.M.S. Rose

from destruction. After the bicentenary the second *Rose* was berthed at Newport but fell into disrepair. In 1984 Kaye Williams purchased her and had her towed to Bridgeport, Connecticut. With the creation of an H.M.S. *Rose* foundation, funds became available for her complete restoration. Work on her was completed in time for the *Rose* to attend the 1986 Statue of Liberty celebrations. The United States Coast Guard has certified the *Rose* as the largest sailing vessel in the United States. She continues to be used for educational sailing trips for trainees on day or overnight trips. Both the *Rose* and the

Bounty attended with other "ships of sail" the 1995 re-enactment of the 1745 siege of Fortress Louisbourg.

Many of those who watched the *Bounty* being built could not but think of another *Bluenose*. After much discussion and thought, the Halifax Oland family, owners of Oland Brewery, accepted the challenge. At the laying of *Bluenose II's* keel on February 27, 1963, Colonel Sidney Oland and marine architect William J. Roue in turn applied a maul to the first spike before the colonel passed it to Captain Angus Walters with the words: "Here Angus. I think you're the one who ought to be doing this!" who finished the task with a skill that belied his eighty-odd-years. Launching day, July 24, 1963, drew thousands. Lieutenant Governor H.P. MacKeen first presented medallions specially struck to mark the occasion. After the Reverend Ralph Webber gave the blessing, Mrs. Sidney Oland christened *Bluenose II* with the traditional bottle of champagne and the words "May God bless and protect this ship and all who sail in her."

The Oland family turned *Bluenose II* over to the province in 1977 to serve as Nova Scotia's ambassador ship. A 1994 refitting has given her a new life as the legend of the original *Bluenose* continues to fascinate succeeding generations.

Bicentenary

In 1953 Lunenburg's population stood at around 3,000; the figure had not significantly changed since the third quarter of the previous century. By 1953, however, the town could boast 700 homes and such civic amenities as a public library, a new hospital called the Fishermen's Memorial Hospital, a curling rink, a hockey arena, tennis and yacht clubs, and a nine-hole golf course.

Bicentennial celebrations began with church services on Sunday morning June 7. In the afternoon there was a combined community religious service in the arena where 1,200 gathered to praise God and to render thanks for 200 years of progress. Then there was an evening performance at the United Church of the oratorio "Elijah," attended by more than a thousand. A pageant re-enacting the first landing of settlers, narrated by Lloyd Crouse, took place the following day. On the Monday evening a massed band concert, with children's choirs from around the county directed Mrs. B.G. Oxner, provided a finale to the celebrations.

Sports and Recreation

In the years following the war, Lunenburg's success on the hockey rink again showed the town's public spiritedness and competitive nature. During the war the Falcons had lost Fred Fox Jr., Harry Fox, Roy Whynacht, Blake Naughler, Mickey Hebb and Ted Montgomery to war service, but the team managed to

Top: Quilt of the Bluenose II by Norma Collier. Above: Painting of the Bluenose by Jack Gray. Both items hang in the foyer of the Maritime Life Building, Halifax.

recruit enough intermediate players to continue playing in a watered-down South Shore League. After the war, among those returning was Fred Fox who had been shot down and become a prisoner of war. He played right up to 1950—a span of 20 years since he first turned out for the Falcons. He continued his support of hockey as a between-periods hockey radio commentator and as president of the South Shore League.

The South Shore League revived in 1946 with Lunenburg, Bridgewater, Chester, Mahone Bay, and Liverpool entering teams. In the semi-finals Lunenburg lost to Chester, which went on to take the title. Although Lunenburgers had gone to play for other teams, the Falcons and other South Shore teams had never relied on imports. This changed with the 1947 season when Chester Basin Red Wings brought in three top players and won the title. Lunenburg did not ice a team in 1948, but in the following year the Falcons decided to import all but two players from Halifax; only Fred Fox and Elvin Ritcey were native Lunenburgers. The Falcons took the South Shore title in 1949 and 1950, but lost in the final to Chester Basin in 1951.

For the 1952 season the Falcons put together one of the strongest teams ever to represent the town. They brought in players who had been in major and senior hockey with some who had come up from junior hockey to the intermediate ranks. The Falcons swept to victory in the South Shore League and then defeated the Antigonish Bulldogs for the Nova Scotia Mainland title. They had little difficulty with the Port Morien Shamrocks for the Nova Scotia championship and the right to play for the Maritime crown. In Fredericton they outclassed the Fredericton Capitals in their series, scoring 14 goals to the Capitals' four and taking the Maritime Intermediate title. The 1953 Falcon team was even stronger, winning the Nova Scotia Senior Championship, but losing to the Saint John Beavers for the Maritime Senior title. In

The Choral Club performing in a play in 1948

these years immediately after the Second World War, Lunenburg could boast the best teams in the town's hockey history.

Hockey teams such as those fielded by Lunenburg and other small towns across the country could not compete for long with televised professional sports. Community team sports went into decline in Lunenburg as elsewhere. More recreational sports like curling and golf have, however, grown greatly in popularity.

The volunteering spirit so noticeable on the home front in both world wars continues today in such community organizations as the Fisherman's Memorial Ladies Hospital Auxiliary, the Boscawen Chapter of the I.O.D.E and Fraternal Orders like the Masons. Remembrance Day ceremonies perpetuate for successive generations a sense of the town's history and its contribution to the cause of peace and freedom. During the province-wide Fire Prevention Week, the town's volunteer Fire Department stages its annual parade.

Since the 1970s an array of cultural societies have come into being that have as their focus heritage preservation, traditional crafts, folk art and music. With the 1977 opening of the Fisheries Museum of the Atlantic on the waterfront, the Lunenburg Heritage Society gained a home for its activities and later so did the South Shore Genealogical Society. Visitors to Lunenburg in the summer months enjoy the Lunenburg Folk Art Festival in early July, followed by the Lunenburg Craft Festival, which draws more than ten thousand people over two days. Then in August there is the Lunenburg Folk Harbour Festival and the Fisheries

Exhibition, which continues to bring thousands to the town. The German-Canadian Cultural Association of Lunenburg County has an Oktoberfest. All these festivals are made possible by the voluntary efforts of citizen committees.

Preserving the Old Town

When Captain William Moorsom visited Lunenburg in 1830 he noted approvingly of its residents' reluctance "to tear down the relics around which long-cherished feeling has wrapped the folds of reverential sanctity." Moreover, Moorsom went on to say "Every householder, from the highest to the lowest, appears to possess the means of keeping his tenement [private residences] in repair and good order; a fact by no means too prevalent in other places." In the last half of the nineteenth century some of the new wealth from shipbuilding, foreign trading and the banks fishery had found expression in constructing New Town. Within the Old Town, though there were some new buildings erected, most owners preferred to renovate. This conservatism meant demolition for new houses was kept to the minimum and the Old Town retained its distinctive architectural heritage.

The bicentenary and the launching of *Bluenose II* increased awareness of the town's history and its heritage buildings. Many residents believed the town should take a more active role in preserving its history. This concern found expression in the organization of the Lunenburg Heritage Society in 1972. From its beginnings the society took an active role in educating fellow citizens in the importance of sound conservation. The society restored several historic houses, inaugurated historic house tours, and placed information plaques on a number of

Above: These Lunenburgers decided to dress up for the 1926 Fishermen's Picnic. In the picture from left to right are John Knickle, the photographer, E.C. Adams, unknown, W.N. Powers, a Mr. Bezanson, Evrett Knickle, Lloyd Crouse, Fred (Scotty) Quinlain, Donald Tanner and the last individual standing is unknown as is the person sitting. Below: The Grade 3 Christmas concert in 1953. Mrs B.G. Oxner, Nancy Zinck (pianist). Front Row: Betty Dauphinee, Joanne Haughn, Pat Tobin, Eugene Schwartz. Standing: Jane Morash, Robert Smith, Barbara Cook, Janet Crouse, Andrew Bald, Sheila Helstrum, Joan Tanner, David Collins, Jane Sterne, Jackie Ritcey, Janice Haughn, Geraldine Corkum, Claire Bailly, Robert Parks

buildings. With the publication in 1979 of *A Walk Through Old Lunenburg*, the society embarked on a publications program. However, neither the society nor the town had any legislative authority for protecting the town's heritage until the passage by the Nova Scotia Legislature of the 1980 *Heritage Property Act*.

After passage of the Act, Lunenburg became one of the first municipalities to enact a heritage by-law, adopted in 1981. In conformity with the Act, the Town Council appointed a Heritage Advisory Committee made up of two council members and interested citizens. This by-law enabled the town to protect designated buildings from substantial exterior alteration and demolition through a registration process under the Act. Since its inception the Heritage Advisory Committee has been very active, meeting ten or twelve times yearly to make recommendations to the Town Council on registrations and requests for exterior alterations, as well as to initiate various heritage conservation projects. By early 1996 the town had 35 properties on its Registry of Heritage Properties. Under the supervision of the Heritage Advisory Committee the town issued a Heritage Advisory Information Kit to guide private owners on appropriate conservation measures.

Among the most effective means used by the Heritage Advisory Committee to raise public awareness about heritage conservation was the 1984 publication of *Lunenburg: An Inventory of Historic Buildings*, compiled by William Plaskett. The town provided each property owner in the Old Town with a free copy. Using informative text and photographs, the publication describes the Old Town's historic buildings.

When the town's high school moved to a new building, the old Lunenburg Academy lost its place as a community centre for educational and cultural activities. If it had not been for the determination of a concerned citizens' group, the building itself might have faced demolition. The founding of Lunenburg Academy Foundation to preserve the building and restore it to its rightful place in the town's life became a practical illustration of the importance that heritage preservation had assumed as a community focus.

Beauty queens from Western Nova Scotian towns on the Nova Scotia Fisheries Exhibition Float in the Fisheries Exhibition parade, c. 1967.

Nationally, the Old Town had long been recognized as having outstanding heritage value to Canadians. A portrait of the waterfront appeared from 1976 to 1995 on the Canadian one hundred-dollar bill. On January 6, 1929 the Post Office issued a fifty-cent commemorative stamp showing the *Bluenose* racing. Since January 1, 1937 she has appeared on one side of the Canadian dime. On the 1995 centenary of the Lunenburg Academy, Canada Post issued a commemorative stamp.

In 1989 the Town Council designated the Old Town as a municipal heritage conservation district. A request followed to the National Historic Sites and Monuments Board of Canada for the Old Town to become a national historic district. In 1991 a comprehensive study of the Old Town's architecture and history was undertaken for the Historic Sites and Monuments Board. Its recommendation led to its 1992 designation as a National Historic District because of the striking historical continuity found in the Old Town's streets, public spaces, buildings, and daily life. National designation gave impetus to the idea for the nomination of Old Town to become a World Heritage Site.

In 1993 the town approached Parks Canada of the Department of Canadian Heritage, which is responsible

for fulfilling Canada's obligations under the United Nations Educational, Scientific and Cultural Organization (UNESCO's) World Heritage Convention. The Convention required a rigorous and lengthy nomination process. Parks Canada supported the nomination and submitted it on behalf of the Government of Canada. The process under the Convention involved a comprehensive analysis to meet the established criteria and included an on-site visit under UNESCO auspices by Professor Roy Graham, professor of architecture at the Catholic University of America, Washington D.C. It was necessary to demonstrate that Old Town Lunenburg was of outstanding universal value under World Heritage

World Heritage Committee designated the Old Town a World Heritage Site in December 1995. It joined the Quebec's Historic District as the only other Canadian designated World Heritage Town; among the few such towns in North America are the historic centres of Mexico City and Old Havana. There are only 469 cultural and natural World Heritage Sites; Lunenburg has become the twelfth Canadian site to receive this honour.

This honour comes when Lunenburg is once again in

Lunenburg Masons posed for this picture in 1958. Front row: Hugh Strachen, Elvin Bailly, Arthur Corkum, Donald Walters, Donald Beck, Jim Kinley, Donald Saul, Reverend Alexander Allen, Russel Orchard, Tom Walters, William Cluett. Back row: John Walters, Lawrence Allen, Fred Chenhall, Hugh H. Corkum, Ray Schwartz, Gorfield Mathews, Al Helstrum, Ross Cook, Donald Collins, Donald Maxner, Clyde Haines, Arthur Risser.

criteria, that it met the "tests of authenticity"— architectural design integrity, consistency in the use of cladding materials over time, high standard of conservation workmanship, and preservation of historic setting—and that its historical resources were being managed in a comprehensive and sensitive manner.

Lunenburg's Old Town met these criteria. UNESCO's

its history facing a challenge to its economic and social well-being. Like so many other small towns there has been an out-migration, particularly of younger people, leaving a population of 2,200, or some 800 less residents than at the town's bicentenary in 1953. Although they have not offset the number leaving, there has been an influx of newcomers seeking a different life style and prepared to invest especially in tourism businesses. But it is the uncertain future of the fishing industry—the mainstay of the town's economic livelihood—that poses the most critical challenge to Lunenburg as pre-eminently a fishing and seafaring community.

Lunenburg, however, has always demonstrated in past periods of bad economic times an impressive ability to marry new innovative fishing methods with aggressive marketing to restore the town's prosperity. Although few among the original settlers had even seen the ocean before leaving their homes for the New World, these landsmen soon mastered the fishing and seafaring skills for which their descendants would become renowned. Local merchants early developed a coasting trade with Halifax, which in the first decades of the nineteenth century, laid the basis for Lunenburg's success in West Indian trading. The result was a "lively and prosperous" town with an enviable reputation for "steady perserverance and systematic economy." When the West

Indian market collapsed in the 1850s, again, merchants like James Eisenhauer found new markets and Captain Benjamin Anderson led the way in developing the banks fishery employing the revolutionary new method of trawling; a half century of prosperity followed. Although there was much resistance to the introduction of trawlers and fresh fish marketing, W.C. Smith & Company and its successor, National Sea Products, persisted and took the industry from its nadir during the Great Depression to the new heights of the 1960s and 1970s.

As the town today faces another period of economic uncertainty and accompanying social change, Lunenburgers can take confidence from how past generations have met similar challenges in an industry that can be bountiful, but always demanding of innovation and fortitude. Lunenburg can enter the twenty-first century with the confident assurance that comes from a history, spanning nearly two and half centuries, whose hallmark is the successful marrying of "enterprise and solidity."

Dory racing in the harbour

Chapter 5

LUNENBURG'S OLD TOWN
A WORLD HERITAGE SITE

L unenburg's Old Town is the best preserved North American example of an eighteenth-century British colonial town plan. This can be seen especially in the striking historical continuity of its geometrically regular streets and blocks, its vernacular architecture, its central public spaces, and in its clear distinction between urban and non-urban spaces. Moreover, the intimate relationship of the Old Town to its waterfront, with its buildings oriented to the harbour, and its dominant hillside setting has remained unchanged from the plan that Surveyor General Charles Morris laid out for the town in 1753. The impressive continuity with the past applies equally and as significantly to the cultural and commercial life of this traditional seafaring and fishing community.

Although the Old Town remains eighteenth century in plan, its architecture is largely nineteenth century. Fully two-thirds of the buildings currently standing date from the nineteenth century. Of the 400 or so Old Town buildings, just eight have been so far confirmed as dating from the last half of the eighteenth century. These are either of the single-storey Cape Cod style or are in the two-storey British Classical tradition, commonly called Georgian. All are of wood with their cladding either shingles or clapboard. In the earliest of these houses their builders used a "coulisse" exterior construction. Builders first set in place vertically grooved or slotted heavy square, upright timbers at the corners and intermediate intervals along the walls and at openings. Into the slots the carpenters then fitted solid planks on edge, one above the other. There is little evidence of coulisse construction in North America

other than Lunenburg, but it may still be found today in parts of Switzerland and Germany whence the original settlers came. Lunenburg Cape Cod style houses usually had between two and four rooms on the ground floor and a sleeping loft in the half-storey upstairs, with a large central hearth for cooking and heat.

The earliest houses are one and one-half storey, low-slung with large central chimneys and their gable roofs parallel to the harbour. Easily recognized characteristics of the single-storey Cape Cod style houses are the tightness of the eaves to the heads of the doors and windows and the low ceilings inside. As the settlement progressed, the austere quality of these first houses gave way to the desire for those built in the British Classical tradition, with their five-bay, two-storey front façades and two large end chimneys. Central doorways with narrow sidelights and transoms and heavy surrounds are a distinguishing feature. The conservative symmetry of this style remained in favour until well into the nineteenth century.

All buildings continued to be clad in wooden clapboards or shingles. When Captain William Moorsom visited in 1830, he commented on the "whimsical" taste of owners in painting their houses white, red, pink, and even green. The small standard lot size contributed to builders following a similar scale in house construction. At mid-century, British Classicism gave way to a mixture of ebullient, adventurous and more ostentatious styles, to satisfy a confident and increasingly prosperous class of ship captains, shipbuilders and merchants. It was fortunate that as this architectural evolution took place the desire for larger houses and lots led to the creation of New

Town, geographically and architecturally distinct from the Old Town. The Old Town thus retained its distinctive eighteenth-century geometrical compact character.

Whatever the eclectic style chosen after the middle of the nineteenth century—the Second Empire with its mansard roof, Victorian Gothic or Italianate—builders often incorporated into their plans what has become the most distinctive characteristic of Lunenburg architecture, the "Lunenburg Bump." This feature drew its inspiration from the five-sided Scottish dormer, which in the hands of Lunenburg builders was extended out and down from the roof to create an overhang or frontpiece above the central doorway. They incorporated this picturesque stylistic bump into the new houses and in the many they remodelled. Owners and their builders seemed to have vied with each other in embodying into their plans a charming variety of the decorative stylistic possibilities inherent in the interplay of bumps and bay windows.

In the twentieth century owners continued to build on empty lots and not tear down older houses. Wood remained the chosen material for cladding. Fewer than one third of the Old Town's buildings date from this century and half of those are from before 1930. Since then perhaps 30 more houses have been built. Owners are more concerned to renovate and to restore. Demolitions have been few. With 90 per cent of properties individually privately owned, standards in sensitive repair and maintenance have continued to remain high, a characteristic of householders that Captain Moorsom commented upon so favourably in 1830. Continuity with the past is also present in the balance of residential to commercial and waterfront buildings which today account for 15 per cent of Old Town's properties.

The Town of Lunenburg's successful submission for the Old Town to become a World Heritage Site concluded that although the Old Town's "plan, architecture and culture are not individually unique, the high level of authenticity of all three elements together is believed to be unique in North America." Visitors to Lunenburg's Old Town can have the pleasure of judging for themselves.

The Romkey House, 80-82 Pelham, as it looked around the turn of this century. Many consider this to be the oldest house in the Old Town.

Chapter 6

A WALKING TOUR
OF THE OLD TOWN

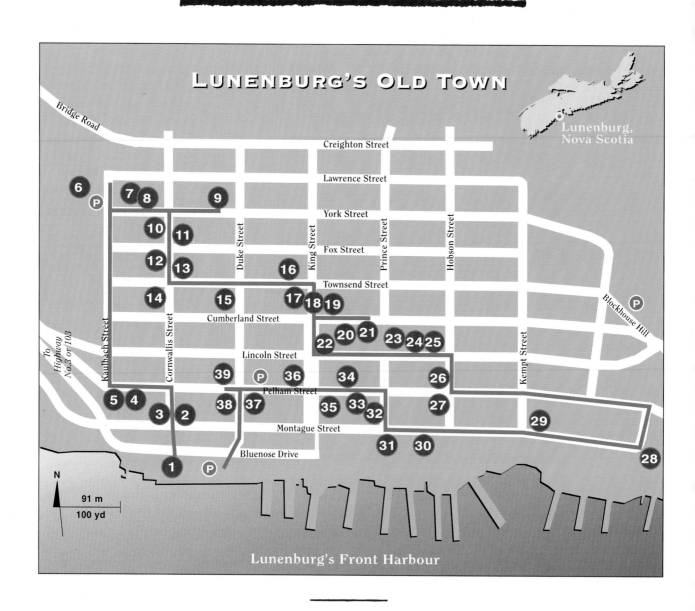

LUNENBURG'S OLD TOWN

Lunenburg,
Nova Scotia

Bridge Road

Creighton Street

Lawrence Street

York Street

Fox Street

Townsend Street

Cumberland Street

Lincoln Street

Pelham Street

Montague Street

Bluenose Drive

Duke Street

King Street

Prince Street

Hobson Street

Kaulbach Street

Cornwallis Street

Kempt Street

Blockhouse Hill

To Highway No.3 or 103

N

91 m
100 yd

Lunenburg's Front Harbour

I suggest you begin your Old Town walk on the waterfront at **68 Bluenose Drive (1)** at the entrance to the **Fisheries Museum of the Atlantic**. You first cross Bluenose Drive and go up a set of stairs to Montague Street at Cornwallis.

At the top right hand corner is the **Morash Gallery, 55 Montague (2)**, built in 1876 by Joseph and Solomon Morash, master carpenters and builders of many of the town's finest residences. Note its hipped gambrel roof, incorporating a two-level bump, and the decorative fret work applied to the second storey window lintels.

Across Cornwallis Street at **53 Montague (3)** is the **George Anderson Sr. House**, c.1850s. The Andersons were one of the few American Loyalist families to come to Lunenburg after the American Revolution.

Now continue up Cornwallis and turn left on Pelham, which will take you to Kaulbach. On Pelham you can see fronting onto that street two other

Anderson family residences. Dating from 1826 is **George Anderson Jr.'s House, 36 Pelham (4)**, while that of **John Anderson, 28 Pelham (5)**, with its

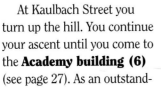

mansard roof and two front bay windows, is 1877.

At Kaulbach Street you turn up the hill. You continue your ascent until you come to the **Academy building (6)** (see page 27). As an outstand-

ing example of late-nineteenth century school architecture it is both a provincially registered property and a National Historic Site, and it is still used as a school.

From the Academy you should double back to York Street. On your immediate left at **43 York (7)** is the **Allan Morash House**, 1888, built, as was the Morash House on Montague Street, by the cousins John and Joseph Morash. Here we

find twin Lunenburg bumps placed on either side of a two-storey frontpiece, itself capped by a bump.

At **57 York (8)** you can see one of the oldest houses,

dating from the 1760s and exhibiting the characteristic one-storey style described above. The oldest part of the house was a "half-Cape" with two windows to one side of the door. A later addition on the other side of the door created the "three-quarter Cape" you see before you.

Across Cornwallis further along York on your left is the attractive **Freeman-Blair House, 89 York (9)**, built between 1828 and 1842. Its massive central chimney is a hold-over from an earlier style, but its classically-inspired five-bay symmetrical

facade and door trim reflect the newer style. From the Freeman-Blair House you should retrace your steps to Cornwallis and proceed down to Fox Street.

At Fox you come to **Zion Lutheran Church (10)**, 1890 (see page 23). Designed in the High Victorian Gothic style, it is richly ornamented with moulded wooden belt and dentil courses, and has a large stained glass memorial window to the Reverend Charles Ernest Cossman. An outstanding feature is

the high tower with its ascending series of mullioned lancet windows and capped by a tall spire, incorporating small louvred gables on all four sides. Zion Lutheran's congregation, the oldest continuing Lutheran congregation in Canada, recently carried out extensive restoration work to the tower.

On the opposite corner at **69 Fox Street** is the

Lennox Tavern (11), saved from certain demolition and painstakingly restored by its present owner. Since 1992 it has been a provincially registered heritage property. Clearly within the classical style it dates from around 1810, when John Lennox erected it as a tavern and inn.

Continuing along you pass a typical late Victorian structure, the **Charles Morash House (12)**, c.1890s, at **66 Fox Street**. Note how the bright yellow paint reinforces the verticality of its architecture.

Facing onto the Parade is **65 Townsend (13)**, one of the most important houses, architecturally and historically. Henry Koch, gentleman and merchant, had the **Koch-Solomon House** built between 1785-97. Its

construction marks the introduction of the British Classical tradition discussed above. In the 1970s its then owner restored it to its original appearance, as you see it today.

Diagonally opposite the Koch-Solomon House is **St. John's Parish Hall (14)**, formerly the town's first court house, 1775, which originally was a five-bay, hipped roof structure with central main door facing Cornwallis Street, but has been much altered over the years. In its main hall hangs a large mural bearing an old Royal Coat of Arms with the inscription *Fist Justitia ruat Caelum* or "Let justice be done though the heavens may fall."

As you turn left along Townsend Street, you enter into the public space that Surveyor General Charles Morris reserved back in 1753, and which still retains its original purpose. On your right is the transformed **St. John's Anglican Church (15)** with its "Carpenter Gothic Style" and sublime interior, the creation of Solomon

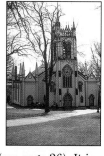

Morash and his shipwright carpenters (see page 26). It is both a provincially registered heritage property and a National Historic Site.

Further on is **St. Andrew's Presbyterian Church (16)**, which has the longest history of any Presbyterian congregation in the nation. Built on the site of the first church in 1828, it was lengthened and Gothicized in 1879 (see page 26). When you come to King Street you can take the stairs between the Town Hall/Court House and the War Memorial leading down to Cumberland Street.

The **Town Hall/Court House (17)** dates from 1893, while the **War Memorial (18)** was unveiled on June 7, 1921, and lists the names of the 37 from the town who died in the First World War. **The Bandstand (19)** is a replica of the 1891 original.

Across the street are the **United Church (20)**, formerly the Methodist Church (see page 26) and opened for services in 1885, and the **Boscawen Inn (21)** at number 150. The inn dates back to 1888 when H.A.N. Kaulbach gave it as a wedding present to his daughter Edna. In the Queen Anne revival style, it has the characteristic asymmetrical lines, emphasized by a circular

tower and projecting bay on the south elevation and an oriel window on the northeast corner. After the Second World War, the west wing was added and the house renovated as a hotel.

You continue down to Lincoln where at **28 King (22)**

is the residence purchased in 1882 by Lunenburg's first mayor, Augustus Wolff (see page 23), with its central "Lunenburg Bump" and two flanking dormers and likely built in 1876.

Further along Lincoln there are three houses of interest. At **315 Lincoln (23)** is **Henry Wilson's residence** which he had built in 1879; it is one of the best preserved examples of Victorian architecture still standing in

Lunenburg. Its large three-storey Italianate frontpiece, incorporating the formal main doorway and high extended dormer, immediately arrests the eye.

Next to it is the house built by **Charles Smith, merchant and mariner, at Number 321 (24)**. Note how, other than the door-

way, its frontpiece resembles that of the Henry Wilson House.

Adjoining it is the 1886 house of **Daniel Rudolf**, merchant and former mayor, **Number 325 (25)**. On this last house note the concave roof over the frontpiece; this feature is unique in the Old Town. From the town's founding, the Rudolf family assumed roles in its political and commercial life.

At Hopson Street you turn down towards the harbour. On Pelham opposite to each other are **Number 163 (26)**, the house of **Lewis Anderson**, an important fish merchant of the 1860s (see page 11), and the **David**

Smith House, Number 166 (27), and dating from 1875-79. David Smith, himself a shipbuilder, was the father of Richard Smith, the founder of the Smith and Rhuland Shipyards, which launched over 200 vessels.

Now turn left onto Pelham, following it to the **Smith and Rhuland's Boatshop (28)** (1947-59) where such replicas as H.M.S. *Bounty* were built (see page 52).

Montague Street will take you back into the Old Town proper.

On Kempt Street corner was formerly **Thomas Walters and Son, Marine and General Blacksmiths (29)**, a fami-

ly business begun in 1893 and as Lunenburg's only blacksmith shop continuously operating until 1995.

Further along, at **170 Montague (30)** on the harbour side, you come to **Adams & Knickle**, ship outfitters; both this firm and Walters and Son provided fittings for *Bluenose II*. The main façade of the Adams & Knickle building is clad in wood

imitative of ashlar.

At the bottom of Prince Street at **144 Montague Street (31)** are the gambrel-roofed buildings of the old **Zwicker Warehouse**.

Turning up Prince takes you past **Number 9**, the **Major Rudolf**

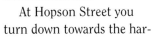

House (32), which may be one of the original houses built during the first summer of settlement in 1753. The dormer is a later addition.

When you come to Pelham, the second in from the corner is **Number 134 Pelham (33)**, known as the **Bailly House**. Among the oldest in the town it dates from the 1760s, though sometime between 1906 and 1914 the roof was changed

from its original gambrel style and raised to give the full two storeys you see today. Earl Bailly, a quadriplegic, lived and had his studio here until his death in 1977. He received international recognition for his oil paintings and watercolours of the town and surrounding countryside.

Farther on at **Number 125** you come to the **Knaut-Rhuland House (34)**, a

provincially registered heritage property. It dates from 1793 and is largely unaltered. As with the Koch-Solomon House, it represents the transition to full Georgian, particularly in its interior layout with its central hall plan. It is the earliest known example in the province of two chimneys inset a quarter distance from the ends of the house, pre-dating by 20 years this Georgian feature found elsewhere. The owners have carried out extensive interior restorations, including using period colours. It is the best preserved example of British Classicism in the Old Town.

The town does not have many stone buildings, but an outstanding exception is the **Bank of Montreal, 12 King Street (35)**. Peden and McLaren of Montreal were the architects in 1907

for this Shelburne grey granite construction. The sensitive

addition by the Halifax firm Duffus, Romans, Single and Kundzins dates from 1966.

At the corner of Pelham and King Streets, at **15 King**, is the **Bolman/Zwicker House**, today the **Compass Rose Inn (36)**. The lawyer Charles Bolman built this house as his residence sometime between 1829 and 1836. Originally it looked much like the Knaut-Rhuland House before later in the century it received the Italiate three-tiered bump. John Zwicker's descendants owned it from 1836 until 1953.

The **Royal Bank of Canada** at **84 Pelham (37)** is of sandstone and dates from 1908.

At **Number 80-82 Pelham** is the **Romkey**

House (38), which is one storey high on the street side but two storeys on the harbour side. Jacob Ushe, a mariner, probably erected it during the period 1779-98, though it could be earlier. It has the solid coulisse construction discussed above and just over six-foot high ceilings. The double leafed door and multi-paned window on the east side of the front elevation date from 1865 when it

became the town's Customs Office.

Diagonally across the street at **75 Pelham** is the **Kaulbach House (39)** now an Historic Inn and a 1995 winner of a Nova Scotia Home Award for Historical Restoration. Dufferin Kaulbach had this house built; it is a fine example of fashionable Lunenburg architecture at the beginning of the 1890s.

From the Romkey House you descend to the harbour front and the **Fisheries Museum of the Atlantic**. The museum is today housed in buildings (1897) used by W.C. Smith and Company and later by National Sea (see page 37).

NOTES

The search for visuals for this book began at the Fisheries Museum of the Atlantic where Heather-Anne Getson not only gave me access to its collections, but kindly read the manuscript, making many valuable comments. The Museum made arrangements so that Wilfred Eisnor of Knickle Studios could photograph various items in its collections. He also provided images from his own studio collection. Heather-Anne also introduced me to Hugh A. Corkum, whose collection made possible the significant number and variety of coloured images in this book.

Others who responded to my call for visual material were Karen Smith of Dalhousie Special Collections, Judy Dietz of the Art Gallery of Nova Scotia, Gordon Fulton of Parks Canada, Bruce Ellis of the Army Museum at the Halifax Citadel, Allison MacDonald of Maritime Life Assurance Company, Gary Shutlak of the Public Archives of Nova Scotia, and Lynn-Marie Richardson of the Maritime Museum of the Atlantic. When I needed photographs of the Lunenburg's first fire engine, among the prized artifacts of the Firefighters' Museum in Yarmouth, Linda Campbell kindly obliged. While we followed my map of the walking tour, Steven Isleifson did the photography. Additional thanks go to Ian Langlands for assistance on National Sea Products. I am grateful to Professor Emeritus J. Murray Beck for reading the manuscript. Without his comments, I would have gone seriously astray on Lunenburg elections.

List of Source Publications

A Walk Through Old Lunenburg, Lunenburg Heritage Society, n.d.

Argus, 1889–1908 and 1923–1933.

Backman, Brian and Phil. *Bluenose*. McClelland and Stewart, Toronto, 1965.

Balcom, Berton. "History of Lunenburg's Bank Fishery Fleet 1873–1933." Dalhousie University, Honours Thesis, Halifax, 1974.

Bell, Winthrop Pickard. *The Foreign Protestants and the Settlement of Nova Scotia*. University of Toronto, 1961.

Colonial Churchman. Lunenburg, 1835–41.

Corkum, Hugh H. *On Both Sides of the Law*. Lancelot, Hantsport, 1989.

Darrach, Claude. *Race To Fame: The Inside Story of The Bluenose*. Lancelot, Hantsport, 1985.

DesBrisay, Mather Byles. *History of the County of Lunenburg,* 1895. Mika Reprint, Belleview, 1980.

Fulton, Gordon. "Old Town Lunenburg, Nova Scotia." Historic Sites and Monuments Board of Canada, Agenda Paper, 1991–22.

Hewitt, H.W. "History of Lunenburg County" unpublished, Public Archives of Nova Scotia.

Kimber, Stephen. *Net Profits*. Nimbus Publishing, Halifax, 1989.

Lunenburg Historic Architecture: A Walking Tour Guide, 1994. Lunenburg Heritage Advisory Committee

Lunenburg Progress. Lunenburg, 1878–1900

MacPherson, Ken and John Burgess. *The Ships of Canada's Naval Forces 1910–93*. Vanwell, St. Catherine's, Ontario, 1994.

Marble, Allen Everett. *Surgeons, Smallpox and the Poor: A History of Medicine and Social Conditions in Nova Scotia, 1749–99*. McGill-Queens, Kingston, 1993.

Plaskett, William. *Understanding Lunenburg Architecture*. 1979, Lunenburg Heritage Society.

Plaskett, William. *An Inventory of Historic Buildings with Photographs and Historical Notes*. 1985.

Progress Enterprise. Lunenburg, 1900–present.

Raddall, Thomas. *West Novas: A History of the West Nova Scotia Regiment*. published by the author, 1947.

"World Heritage List Nomination for Old Town Lunenburg." Department of Canadian Heritage and Municipality of Lunenburg, 1994.

INDEX